CUISINE
NATURELLE

CUISINE NATURELLE

Anton Mosimann

Atheneum   New York   1986

Photographs by John Lee
Illustrations by Jane Human

Library of Congress Cataloging-in-Publication Data

Mosimann, Anton.
Cuisine naturelle.

Includes index.
1. Cookery (Natural foods) I. Title.
TX741.M67 1985   641.5   85-47610
ISBN 0-689-11587-3

En hommage à tous ceux qui m'ont
appris à devenir Cuisinier

ACKNOWLEDGMENTS

I would like to say thank you particularly to Dr. Janet Gale, lecturer in health and social welfare at the Open University, and also to Lyn Hall (principal of La Petite Cuisine School of Cooking), Cherry Stevens, Jane Suthering, Sylvia Baumann, Christiane Schröder, Kit Chan, Roy Raiman, Ralph Bürgin, Ian Champion, Michael Bonacini, Clive Howe and to the Dorchester Hotel and the Kitchen Brigade.
And a special thank you to Susan Fleming, who edited *Cuisine Naturelle*. She is a brilliant editor, and without her help I could not have completed this book.

CONTENTS

CUISINE NATURELLE

INTRODUCTION

The pleasures given by a carefully prepared and beautifully presented meal are joyful and unique experiences in themselves. Everyone—old or young, rich or poor—wishes to eat food that is flavorful, original, and exciting, however simple that basic food may be. Eating is something that people do two or three times a day, basically for the purpose of sustaining life, and the preparation for eating merits all the care, love, and creativity the cook can lavish upon it.

My philosophies of food and life are the same. Both should be experiences of happiness, serenity, and joyful giving. The health of the mind depends on maintaining interest, on being happily and constructively occupied; the physical health of the body depends on controlled exercise, which in turn leads to alertness of mind. The health of both mind and body is dependent ultimately on how we eat. We are undoubtedly, to a certain extent, composed of what we eat—and excess of certain foods or basic ingredients can influence physical and mental states and capacities.

Fortunately, we can create a balance, whereby good food and good living go hand in hand, a balance that is not in the least difficult to attain. For if moderate amounts of food—the best seasonal vegetables and fruit, the most beautiful of fish, the leanest slices of meat, the least fatty of dairy produce—are prepared with delicacy and eaten with wholehearted appreciation, we could all be of better temper, more mentally alert, healthier, and could grow with a happiness of spirit, balanced both mentally and physically.

To prepare a meal carefully, with the best ingredients and only the well-being of your guests in mind, is to give them a special gift—not only the gift of a memorable meal, but also the gift of life. In the recipes that follow in this book, I shall show you how to prepare food for life, simply cooked and creatively presented, to encourage good temper, long life, and much happiness.

What Is Cuisine Naturelle?

In the past, "good food" and "food that is good for you" were often seen as mutually exclusive: food could be either one or the other but never appeared to be both. And yet there is no valid reason why there should be any contradiction between eating well and eating healthily. The basic principles of good cooking—and my own style of cooking—have always been to use the freshest, most perfect ingredients and to prepare them in the way best suited to them—simply, subtly, to bring out color, flavor, succulence, and goodness. To these principles I have added an extra dimension—the ideas behind Cuisine Naturelle—to create a new unity and balance: the pleasure of enjoying the finest food and cuisine while nurturing the health of the body.

Today, in a Western world newly conscious of the relationship between health and food, people are worried about four main health problems:

○ diseases arising from overweight
○ heart disease and problems of the circulatory system
○ problems of the stomach and digestive system
○ dental problems

The most controllable dietary culprits that are believed to cause or to exacerbate these problems are excessive fats, oils, salt, sugar, and caloric intake, as well as insufficient intake of dietary fiber, fresh fruits, and vegetables.

Cuisine Naturelle is therefore characterized first by the exclusion of many of these ingredients. In my recipes I use no oil, butter, cream, or alcohol and none of the cooking methods or techniques that require their use. I have also carefully reduced the need for salt and sugar, and as a result of all these exclusions and reductions, the caloric value of many dishes is decreased. By quick and careful choice and preparation of many ingredients—vegetables in particular—dietary fiber and essential nutrients are retained fully for the use of the body.

Exclusions

Butter, oils, cream, and alcohol do undoubtedly have their rightful place in good cooking and haute cuisine—contributing to many fine, classic dishes, adding flavor and indeed goodness (for none is essentially *bad*)—but they can have deleterious effects as well. Butter, oils, and cream contain fats, which increase calorie and cholesterol consumption—both undesirable for the weight- and health-conscious (cholesterol is directly related to artery and thus heart and circulatory problems)—and alcohol not only contains sugar and calories but also can affect the liver and increase blood pressure.

When possible, therefore, low-fat equivalents of traditional ingredients have been substituted if necessary—natural yogurt, fromage blanc, and tofu (soybean curd) instead of cream, for instance—and sauces (often said to be the ultimate test of a chef) are based not on butter, cream, or alcohol reductions but on good stocks of meat, fish, or vegetables or colorful vegetables or fruits. Recipes are given for making many of the above equivalents, but selected commercial varieties, provided that you choose those that contain no coloring, preservatives, and the like, could be used instead.

As a result, the visual effect of many dishes is lighter, clearer, with outlines and colors not muted by cream or butter. The natural flavors of many foods, too, are more honest, more *real,* not overpowered by sauces made with alcohol, and the overall experience is thus more carefully focused, defined, and enhanced.

Reductions

The exclusion of cream, butter, and oils ensures an immediate reduction in the fat content of many foods that already contain fat—even lean meat, for instance, contains some 20 percent fat. By carefully preparing meat—by cutting away visible fat and choosing the leanest cuts (as in the following recipes)—a further reduction is obtained.

But Cuisine Naturelle is not designed to be a dogmatic or extreme form of cooking or eating. Some fat in the diet is necessary so that fat-soluble vitamins, such as A, E, K, and D, can be absorbed in our bodies. Salt, too, which, in excess, contributes to high blood pressure and strokes, is a mineral needed by the body in small amounts, which vary according to climatic and other conditions. It is required in cookery as well, to set the nutrients in green vegetables, for instance, and, primarily, to season and give flavor. Foods without any salt would not taste so good, but quantities can be reduced, and I have also created some herb mixtures (see page 36) which, when added to a recipe, can reduce the need for salt in that recipe by about 50 percent.

Sugar, too, is the "white death" for many present-day writers on health. It undeniably adds nothing nutritionally to the body except calories, and so my recipes use considerably less. (Artificial sweeteners must never be used because some can be harmful to health—and taste unpleasant as well.) Many of the recipes that require sugar, the desserts, rely more on the natural sweetness of the major ingredient, normally fruit.

The overall effect of the reductions that characterize Cuisine Naturelle is to reduce caloric intake and create a new balance of health-promoting ingredients, which favor a higher proportion of natural fiber and lower amounts of potentially harmful ingredients.

The most basic reduction of all, perhaps, is that of quantity of food. Portions are designed not to overwhelm the eater but to look delicate and inviting, to whet and satisfy the appetite—not challenge it to a duel! Appetizers are often served as main dishes (which is why that chapter is the longest in the book), accompanied by vegetables and garnishes served on the same plate (sensible because everything keeps considerably warmer and looks absolutely freshly prepared).

Basic Methods of Preparation

The second major characteristic of Cuisine Naturelle must be the methods of preparation themselves. To practice that art properly, the cook not only should be enthusiastic, dedicated, and continually creative but must also be aware of the "scientific" basis of the art—why food acts and reacts in the way that it does. The cook must understand the structure of food, judge its qualities through the senses of smell and taste, and creatively apply that knowledge, first of all, to the methods of preparation.

Most classical cooking methods can be adapted, with the obvious exceptions of fat-based roasting and deep-fat and pan-frying. Steaming, poaching, broiling, and dry sautéing are the basics—all of them quick—for preserving flavor, texture, color, nutrients, and, above all, the qualities of the foods themselves. Broiling needs no added fat because of the intrinsic fats of meat or fish; sautéing, to sear, sweat, or brown ingredients, is done carefully in a dry, nonstick pan, again relying on the hidden fat of meat and the moisture content of vegetables; steaming and poaching are already well known as healthy, controllable methods of preparing food so that their nutrients can be fully taken up and used by the body.

Whichever method is used, it must be done carefully and lovingly, to just the right stage, to retain the valuable properties of the food. Fine cooking must preserve the qualities of fine ingredients.

Ingredients

The basis of fine cuisines all over the world is to be found in the careful selection and correct preparation of excellent ingredients—and the same is, of course, true of Cuisine Naturelle. Choose the freshest seasonal vegetables from the market; the freshest fish (after visiting Billingsgate fish market in London, I cannot wait to return to the kitchen to produce a dish that will do justice to the turbot, lobster, or other fish that I have just personally selected); the finest meats or free-range poultry. In fact, throughout the recipes I have tried to avoid the adjective "fresh"; the foods used in Cuisine Naturelle *are,* and *must be,* fresh.

All canned, processed, or factory-produced foods should be avoided. And, although often less easy to obtain, it is undoubtedly true that the best meats are those from animals fed properly, not chemically fattened. Personally, I prefer organically grown vegetables and fruit, and the free-range egg just *tastes* better than that from the mass-produced "factory" chicken (unless the chicken has found wild garlic to feed on!).

The raw materials produced by nature are in themselves the finest food, and retaining their original taste is one of the most important principles of Cuisine Naturelle. The good cook should always follow the axiom formulated by the great chef Auguste Escoffier: "La bonne cuisine est celle où les choses ont le goût de ce qu'elles sont" (Good cooking is that in which things taste of what they are). It is to that principle above all others—as you will see from the recipes to follow—that I have dedicated my professional life and this book.

The Presentation

The presentation of any dish, and no less in Cuisine Naturelle, is basic to its enjoyment. The simplest of foods can be placed on the plate to enhance its natural grace, as well as to increase the diner's appetite. For instance, a poached fillet of fish garnished with a few fresh herbs and colorful vegetables can please the eye as well as the stomach—for the part played by the senses of sight and smell is probably still undervalued in stimulating the gastric juices. It is never necessary to have an elaborate presentation.

Sauces and other garnishes and accompaniments, too, add to the visual effect of a dish as well as to its taste (although in general fewer sauces are used in Cuisine Naturelle). A simply grilled chicken breast, arranged on a natural, interestingly seasoned vegetable sauce, is a delight to the eye and ultimately to the palate.

And the plate or dish on which the food is arranged is important, too. The best plates upon which to present food are the plainest—the food should be the picture, not the plate. As you will see from the photographs throughout the book, we have used plain black and plain white plates, which are a wonderful canvas on which to "paint" with vivid vegetable and fruit colors.

Menu Planning

This is largely a matter of combining ideas with a large proportion of common sense.

Cooking and eating should be interesting, exciting, and different. In fact, the art of cooking is just that: no dishes turn out exactly the same twice, and a new sauce or dish may be created by accident. The cook is, in essence, continually an apprentice, constantly sampling, trying again, learning.

Thus a menu should also be interesting, exciting, and different. The ingredients for courses should differ in content for interest and nutritional balance—a fresh appetizer should be followed by a main course of meat or poultry; the textures should excite—no two courses should contain a mousseline, for instance, and crisp vegetables can complement a soft-fleshed fish; the methods of preparation should be varied to create interest—try to avoid two or more courses that are steamed or sautéed.

Color, too, is a vital ingredient of menu planning and makes a vital contribution to the finished look and balance of a meal: plan colors carefully, set off a poached white chicken breast with a green vegetable and a red garnish rather than a white purée of celeriac, say; and follow with a richly colored fruit dessert rather than a (white again) vanilla pudding or ice cream.

Tastes, too, are obviously vital to the success of a dish or a meal—and an imaginative cook is continually experimenting, marrying flavors, to create something new and different (although a good cook, while knowing when to innovate, when to improve, will also know when to leave well enough alone). Try to include and mix the flavors of sweet, salt, sour, and bitter to achieve a good flavor balance: offset the bitterness of brussels sprouts or chicory with a little reduced apple juice, for instance, to get an ideal medium.

Taste can be like color. Some people like red, some like blue—neither is right or wrong—and the same applies to taste. Many people just do not *like* a particular taste or taste combination. An important feature of good menu planning—though often disregarded—is not only to be able to recognize good combinations of tastes but to remember and respect the tastes of the guests.

Perhaps one of the most important things to remember about menu planning is *not* to plan too meticulously. The good, creative cook should never have set ideas when shopping for the basic ingredients of his or her art—but should buy what is best, what is good that day. You may not have planned to buy melons, but if they look, feel, and *smell* good and seem better than your original choice of fruit, change those plans and adapt. The essential ingredient, in effect, is flexibility.

The Philosophy of Cuisine Naturelle

"Healthy" food does not mean a joyless life of deprivation. On the contrary, I want to celebrate the delights and pleasures of eating food that is light and wholesome and looks irresistible. Cuisine Naturelle is *happy* food, and it was created to ally my basic principles of good cooking to those of good nutrition and health. I was helped enormously in this by two good friends—Dr. Janet Gale, who devised and advised on the health and nutrition side, and Lyn Hall, principal of La Petite Cuisine School of Cooking, whose expertise enlightened the photographic sessions—and I am very grateful to them both.

No longer will it be necessary to pay dearly in terms of health to enjoy good cooking. Cuisine Naturelle has married the two, and I hope that the ideas and recipes on the following pages will bring much happiness to all those who—like me—enjoy living well, eating well, and *staying* well.

ANTON MOSIMANN

THE BASICS OF
CUISINE NATURELLE

By the basics of Cuisine Naturelle are meant the methods of preparation, the methods of cooking—although the words *to cook* are often misused in the kitchen (there are only a few raw materials that are *cooked*). Anyone who is fully familiar with all these basic methods of preparation—who can understand them, apply them, and use them correctly—can cook anywhere in the world, for they are the multiplication tables of cooking.

Cuisine Naturelle, by its very nature, does not use some methods of basic preparation—those that need oils or butter for success, like roasting or deep-frying, for instance—while many others have been adapted. The following are the major methods of preparation relevant to Cuisine Naturelle.

Blanching
Blanchir

 Blanching means to treat food with boiling water to whiten it, preserve its natural color, loosen the skin, or remove a strong flavor or smell. The food can be brought rapidly to the boil in cold water and boiled for a short time, or it can be plunged into boiling water. In both instances, the food must be placed quickly thereafter in cold or ice water to prevent further cooking. Blanching is usually a preliminary to other cooking methods.

Vegetables   Place in rapidly boiling, lightly salted water and bring back to the boil. Drain quickly and plunge into cold water (or cold vegetable stock for added flavor). Remove and use as required. This method guarantees that the chlorophyll-related vitamins and mineral salts are retained in green vegetables. This is also vital before freezing vegetables because it inactivates enzymes and sets the color.

Blanching also softens marginally, as with salad leaves to be used as a wrapping, and it is useful for removing peel or skin, as with tomatoes. It can also remove the strong flavor of some vegetables—such as peppers, celery, cauliflower, or onions—at the same time making some of them more easily digestible.

Potatoes should be placed in deep boiling salted water and brought to the boil. Remove potatoes quickly and allow to cool on a rack or a towel.

Fruit   Blanching in boiling water for a couple of seconds helps remove the skin from peaches, for instance.

Meat and Meat Bones for Stocks   These should always be blanched before further preparation. Bring to the boil in cold water. This opens the pores or cells, removing impurities.

Blanching firms up some foods, like sweetbreads, before further preparation. Bring to the boil in cold water before plunging into more cold water.

Chicken Bring to the boil in cold water for white poultry stock. Drain and continue as required.

Blanching Essentials

○ A saucepan large enough to hold what you wish to blanch—a whole chicken or a large quantity of chopped bones—is necessary.

○ Another large container is needed to hold cold water into which to plunge the food after blanching.

○ Cool the blanched food quickly, using ice perhaps. Food needs to be brought down to below 68° F as rapidly as possible to prevent bacterial contamination or spoilage.

Poaching
Pocher

Poaching is a gentle and protective method of food preparation, which is done in a liquid or in a container in a bain-marie at 150 to 175° F. Poaching can also be achieved in a double boiler. The food must be submerged or partially submerged in liquid, and that liquid should barely move. If the temperature of the poaching medium rises above 175° F, the protein of the food begins to break down.

Poached food, like steamed food, retains flavor, texture, and nutrients to a high degree.

Poaching in Liquid Fish above all benefits from the poaching method, in a little liquid or in a court bouillon. Poultry, after being blanched, can be poached in white poultry stock. Variety meats, too, benefit from poaching, and eggs are, of course, the original poached food (the word *poach* comes from the French for pocket, meaning the coagulated white surrounding the yolk like a pocket).

Poaching in a Bain-Marie Vegetables, terrines, eggs, custards, and desserts can be poached in containers in a bain-marie.

Poaching in a Double Boiler The same temperature applies to poaching in a double boiler or a bowl suspended over "quivering" water in a pan. This method is used for sauces that require the gentlest of heating.

Poaching Essentials

○ A pan large enough for the process is vital—for a whole fish, for instance.

○ The poaching liquid—water, stock, or court bouillon—must barely quiver: if it bubbles all over the pan, it is boiling.

○ If poaching in a bain-marie, either on top of or in the oven, make sure the water level cannot reach the top of the individual containers. A roasting tray with small containers, like ramekins, makes an effective bain-marie.

○ Many poached foods benefit from being left in the poaching liquid to cool, so they retain their tenderness and juiciness fully.

Simmering
Bouillir lentement

Simmering is the method of preparation between poaching and boiling, when the liquid is at a temperature of about 203° F.

Meat   For boiled meat, lamb, veal, or tongue, start off with lightly salted water or stock, possibly blanching first. Bring to the boil and then allow to simmer. Do not cover.

Clear Broths and Stocks   Start off with cold water or stock to extract the flavor, and then simmer. To obtain a clear broth, and to avoid the breakdown of protein, the casserole or pot should never be covered.

Simmering Essentials
- Any good strong saucepan will be suitable for simmering.
- The liquid should tremble only, with merely the slightest movement on the surface.

Boiling
Cuire

Food may be cooked in boiling water or stock to required tenderness—although many so-called boiled foods are boiled for only a short time before being simmered. Meat and poultry would toughen if boiled, and fish would break up if boiled throughout the entire cooking time. Boiled beef, for instance, is simmered for the majority of the cooking time after an initial boiling. Boiling can often result in a considerable loss of nutritive value because many nutrients are thrown away in the cooking liquid.

Boiling is mainly used for pasta, rice, and dry vegetables. The working temperature is 212° F.

Boiling Vegetables   Potatoes and root vegetables should be started off in cold water and covered.

Green vegetables should be started off in lightly salted boiling water, in a proportion of one part vegetables to three of water, and preferably left to boil with the lid off. This cooks the vegetables more quickly and retains more vitamins, minerals, and color.

Boiling Pasta   Pasta should be started off in hot, slightly salted water and left uncovered, cooking rapidly. Pasta must be cooked *al dente,* in a proportion of 1 to 10 of water.

Boiling for Reducing   Boiling is also used, particularly in Cuisine Naturelle, to reduce liquids rapidly for stocks and sauces. The rapid boiling in an uncovered pan evaporates some of the liquid, thus thickening the consistency and concentrating the flavor.

Boiling Essentials
- The liquid must be at a rolling boil, with bubbles all over the surface.
- At all times, follow instructions on whether or not to cover the pan. Never cover pasta, for instance, because it boils over very quickly and becomes floury.

○ When reducing, salt *after* reduction, not before, because the saltiness can also become concentrated.

Steaming
Cuire à la vapeur

There are three basic methods: the quick steaming of vegetables, meat, or fish in direct contact with steam produced by boiling liquid beneath; the prolonged, gentle steaming of sweet or savory puddings, say, where the food does not come in direct contact with the steam; and steaming under pressure as in a pressure cooker. The first is the method most relevant to Cuisine Naturelle: no fat or sauce needs to be added to the food, and fatless food is much easier to digest as well as being much more healthy.

Steaming food over boiling water—or court bouillon or any other aromatic infusion—is more delicate and more controllable than other processes. Instead of rolling around in liquid as in boiling, foods are stationary, thus less likely to overcook or break up, and are heated gently by the condensation of steam from the boiling liquid. A major advantage is that the water that condenses and drips back dissolves out fewer minerals, vitamins, and natural flavors than are lost in boiling. The liquid over which the food has steamed should be used in stocks, soups, and sauces.

Because steaming is so quick and delicate, it is ideal for fish and shellfish and for vegetables of all kinds. Meat, poultry, potatoes, and rice may also be steamed very successfully.

Steaming Essentials

○ Special steamers are available, but many can be improvised. A large pot with a well-fitting lid (or use foil as well to ensure a good fit) is vital so that there is room for plenty of liquid, thus plenty of steam. A strainer, colander, or something like a drum-sieve to fit onto the rim of the pot, or to suspend from the rim, is the next requirement; often a grid or rack that will fit in the pot and that can stand above the water level will be more appropriate.

○ The water must not touch the equipment holding the food. It must boil constantly to produce steam, and it should be watched to avoid boiling dry (have extra stock or boiling water nearby to maintain liquid level). The working temperature is that of boiling water, 212° F. (Under pressure the temperature of the steam reaches 400 to 425° F. Cooking times should be reduced if a pressure cooker is used.)

Sautéing
Sauter

Conventionally, foods are sautéed in a little fat; in Cuisine Naturelle no fat is used, and good nonstick pans are vital pieces of equipment. For some foods, like strips of meat, an initial high heat is necessary to sear the outside to retain the juices. The pan must be moved constantly to keep the food moving; or the food itself may be moved with a wooden implement, as in stir-frying. For other foods, like onions or vegetables, a lower temperature is required, so that the substance is "sweated" and does not brown. Move the food constantly, and maintain the process until it reaches the desired tenderness—still *al dente* for many vegetables, soft and transparent for onions and shallots.

Foods that can be sautéed include onions, vegetables, potatoes, small pieces of meat, poultry, or fish, as well as steaks, cutlets, poultry and game breasts, and fish fillets.

Sautéing Essentials

○ The nonstick pans *must* be of very good and heavy quality—cheaper, thinner pans would scorch. Always use wooden or rubber implements so that the nonstick coating is not damaged.

○ Foods to be sautéed should be quite dry, and the pan should not be overcrowded; otherwise the food might steam, poach, or simmer, not brown.

○ Sautéing needs constant attention because many foods could brown too quickly and burn, and many could go beyond the desired pink and tender stage (poultry breasts, for example).

○ When sautéing meat, sharply falling temperatures must be avoided or the meat loses too many of its juices and becomes tough.

Grilling
Griller

Grilling is a very healthy method of preparation and can be carried out with either top or bottom open heat. Grilling over charcoal—or over mesquite—lends a particular characteristic taste to the food. A high heat should be used at the beginning to close the pores of the food (between 430 and 500° F), and then the heat should be lowered (to between 300 and 410° F) to grill to desired degree of doneness. Use a high heat for smaller, thinner pieces of food, a more moderate heat for large pieces.

Grilling is suitable for small and medium-sized fish, for pieces of meat such as steaks, cutlets, chops, and variety meats, and for poultry, game, and vegetables. The process is quick and healthy, most of the fat content dripping into the grill pan beneath. No *added* fat is necessary because of the fat already within many foods to be grilled.

Grill vegetables at a lower heat than meat because they are smaller in size and will burn quickly.

Grilling Essentials

○ The grill must be preheated to its highest level so that the juices of the food may be sealed in immediately.
○ Follow grilling instructions in individual recipes; timing is very important.
○ Turn food over with tongs or two spoons (fish with fish slicers) because piercing with a fork will allow juices to escape.

Gratinéeing
Grainer

In this process finished dishes are browned or glazed in the oven or under the grill at a high temperature with the heat coming from above (approximately 480 to 570° F). Often the dishes are covered with a mixture—bread crumbs, cheese, or some other ingredient—that will brown or crisp under the heat. For many uncooked foods with a porous structure, gratinéeing at a slightly lower temperature can be the entire cooking process.

Foods that can be gratinéed are soups, fish, meat, poultry, vegetables, potatoes, and pasta.

Gratinéeing Essentials

○ Care must be taken not to *burn* rather than brown the topping or top of the dish.
○ Timing is important, or an already finished dish may be *over*grilled or overbaked.

Baking in the Oven
Cuire au four

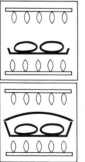

Baking differs from modern roasting only in that food is put into the hot closed oven to bake in a dry heat, *without* added fat. The term is almost synonymous in English with baking bread, cakes, and pastries in an oven, but the application is much wider: many other foods can be baked, and the method is particularly suitable for meat, poultry, and fish dishes (many of which can be baked in a pastry, foil, or other covering), for potatoes, vegetables, and pasta dishes, and for pastries and desserts. Foods can be baked in ovenproof and nonstick molds or dishes or on nonstick baking sheets and at a temperature range from 285 to 480° F.

Oven-Baking Essentials

○ The oven temperature stated in the recipe must be followed for complete success, particularly with breads, and the like. If unsure of the efficacy of your oven, use an oven thermometer to measure its temperature.
○ Use good-quality nonstick bakeware.

Stewing
Étuver

Stewing is the method used to prepare meat, vegetables, or fruit in a firmly covered stewing pot or pan, at a lower temperature than boiling. It is in effect much the same as simmering. Without the help of butter or fat, Cuisine Naturelle stewing must start off with an initial quick sautéing (for meat, to sear), or sweating to release juices (as from onions). Liquid such as stock may be added, and the food is covered and stewed at a low temperature of about 230 to 275° F. As little liquid as possible should be used in most cases because the stewing process also involves steam or condensation, and so that the gravy or stock may become thick. Depending on the dish, the stock may be served as well.

Stewing is a healthy way of preparation because it retains all the vitamins and minerals of the food within the covered pot. It is particularly suitable for fish, small pieces of meat such as veal, vegetables such as mushrooms, and fruit.

Stewing Essentials

○ A good heavy casserole with a tightly fitting lid is vital.
○ A slow, gentle heat must be maintained, whether stewing in or on top of the oven.

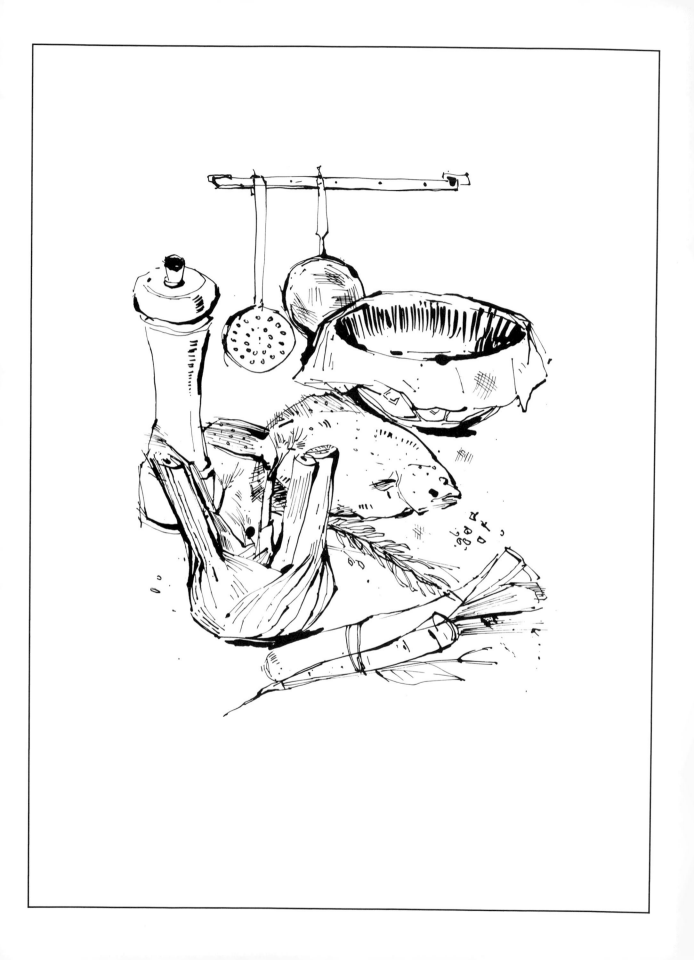

STOCKS AND SAUCE BASES

A good rich stock is one of the most important elements in fine cooking—for soups, sauces, and many other uses—but it is even more important in Cuisine Naturelle, which lacks the flavors usually contributed by the excluded ingredients.

Stocks must be lovingly and carefully prepared. The best and freshest ingredients are vital, the bones should always be cut up small, all fat should be removed, and stock making should never be hurried. This latter is particularly true of reductions of stock: this process recurs frequently throughout the recipes because reduced stock takes the place of oils in dressings and other sauces.

Stocks should never be covered, or they will become cloudy. They should be strained carefully—through a fine cloth or sieve—and the liquid should *drip* into the container beneath. Never force the liquid through by pressing the stock ingredients, and the bottom of the cloth or sieve must not touch the strained liquid in the container.

If a stock looks cloudy, it may be clarified in two ways—with the white of an egg or with ice.

To clarify with egg white, mix a lightly beaten egg white with a few ice flakes or cubes and add to the warm stock. Bring to the boil, stirring constantly. The egg white will coagulate, trapping the small particles that cause the cloudiness, and the stock will become noticeably clearer. Strain through a cheesecloth-lined sieve.

To clarify with ice, stir some ice flakes or cubes into the warm stock and bring to the boil, stirring constantly. The coldness of the ice will cause the solid particles to come together. Strain through a cheesecloth-lined sieve.

Also in this section are a few of the most fundamental of Cuisine Naturelle sauce bases. These are yogurt, yogurt curd cheese, quark, and fromage blanc, and they are used throughout the recipes for taste, texture, and thickening instead of butter and cream. All are low in fat and are fairly simple to make at home.

Whether simple or complicated, sauces demand a great deal of care and practice. The new art of cooking presents sauces which are light and delicate, have their basis in the individual dish itself, and almost all of which are made without flour. Many are made from a simple purée of vegetables, and Cuisine Naturelle sauces are, of course, made without butter or cream, relying instead on reductions of good stocks. Most of the sauces throughout the book appear with the recipe for which they are intended.

Included in this section are recipes for filo dough—the only pastry to feature in Cuisine Naturelle dishes because it is so light and contains no fat—and a basic recipe for ravioli dough.

Fundamental to the ideas of Cuisine Naturelle is the reduction of salt. The herb mixtures—for fish, meat, poultry, and game—will help cut down on salt consumption. They add flavor without overpowering, and their use can cut the potential salt content of a dish by half.

MEAT BROTH
Bouillon de viande

To give the broth a good color, the onion is browned in its skin. Dry sauté in a nonstick pan or directly on a griddle or similar surface until brown but not cooked.

MAKES ABOUT 1 QUART

2 to 2¼ pounds	raw beef bones, chopped and blanched
About ½ pound	raw lean beef trimmings
8 cups	water
2 ounces	bouquet garni (leek, carrots, clove, celeriac, and parsley stems tied together)
½	browned onion (see above)
	Salt and freshly ground pepper

○ Place the soaked and blanched bones and meat in cold water in a saucepan. Bring to the boil and skim.

○ Add the remaining ingredients.

○ Simmer for 2 hours, occasionally skimming and removing the fat.

○ Strain the broth through cheesecloth or a fine sieve, allowing it to drip, and season to taste.

WHITE POULTRY STOCK
Fond blanc de volaille

This white stock is used for poaching chicken and for white chicken and other sauces. The stewing hen can be used afterward for various cold dishes such as salads and mousses.

MAKES ABOUT 1 QUART

1	stewing hen, blanched
8 cups	water
1	white bouquet garni (onion, white of leek, celeriac, and herbs, tied together)
	Salt and freshly ground pepper

○ Put the stewing hen in a large saucepan, fill with the cold water, bring to the boil, and skim.

○ Add the bouquet garni and seasoning.

○ Simmer gently for 2 hours, occasionally skimming and removing the fat.

○ Strain the stock through cheesecloth or a fine sieve, allowing it to drip, and season to taste.

WHITE VEAL STOCK
Fond blanc de veau

Calves' feet and/or veal trimmings may be used instead of, or as well as, veal bones.

MAKES ABOUT 1 QUART

2 pounds	raw veal bones, cut into small pieces and blanched
8 cups	water
1	white bouquet garni (onion, white of leek, celeriac, and herbs, tied together)
	Salt and freshly ground pepper

○ Place the blanched bones in cold water, bring to the boil, and skim.

○ Add the bouquet garni and seasoning.

○ Simmer for 2 hours, occasionally skimming and removing the fat.

○ Strain the stock through cheesecloth or a fine sieve, allowing it to drip, and season to taste.

BROWN POULTRY STOCK
Fond brun de volaille

This brown stock is used for brown chicken sauces. The color and
strength come from the repeated reduction.

MAKES ABOUT 1 QUART

2 to 2¼ pounds	poultry bones and trimmings, cut into small pieces
⅓ cup	mirepoix (diced carrots, onions, celeriac, and herbs)
⅓ cup	diced tomatoes
8 cups	water
	Salt and freshly ground pepper

○ Roast the bones and trimmings in a roasting pan in a moderate oven (325° F)
until brown.

○ Remove the fat with a spoon or strain off. Add the mirepoix and tomatoes and
continue to roast carefully for a further 4 to 5 minutes.

○ Remove from the oven and transfer to a saucepan.

○ First, add 2 cups of water, bring to the boil, and reduce to a glaze.

○ Add the same amount of water again and reduce to a glaze.

○ Add the remaining water and simmer carefully for 2 hours, occasionally skimming
and removing the fat.

○ Strain through cheesecloth or a fine sieve, allowing it to drip, and season to taste.

BROWN VEAL STOCK
Fond brun de veau

MAKES ABOUT 1 QUART

2 to 2¼ pounds	raw veal bones and trimmings, cut into small pieces
⅓ cup	mirepoix (diced carrots, onions, celeriac, sprigs of rosemary, and thyme)
1 pound	tomatoes, diced
6 cups	white veal stock (see page 20)
4 cups	water
	Salt and freshly ground pepper

○ Roast the veal bones and trimmings in a roasting pan in a moderate oven (325° F) until brown.

○ Remove the fat with a spoon or strain off, then add the mirepoix and tomatoes, and roast for another 4 to 5 minutes.

○ Remove from the oven and transfer to a saucepan.

○ Add half the clear white stock, bring to the boil, and reduce by half.

○ Add the remaining stock and reduce to a glaze, about 10 to 12 minutes.

○ Add the water and simmer for 2 hours, occasionally skimming and removing the fat.

○ Strain through cheesecloth or a fine sieve, allowing it to drip, and season to taste.

LAMB STOCK
Fond d'agneau

Lambs' feet or raw lamb trimmings can also be used with, or instead of,
the lamb bones.

MAKES ABOUT 1 QUART

2 to 2¼ pounds	raw lamb bones, chopped finely and blanched
8 cups	water
1	white bouquet garni (onion, white of leek, celeriac, and herbs, tied together)
	Some parsley stems
	Salt and freshly ground pepper

○ Put the blanched bones into the cold water, bring to the boil, and skim.

○ Add the bouquet garni, parsley stems, and seasoning.

○ Allow to simmer for 1 hour, occasionally removing the fat and skimming.

○ Strain the stock through cheesecloth, allowing it to drip, and season to taste.

GAME STOCK
Fond de gibier

Any game bird can be used, depending on the recipe for which it is required. By means of repeated reduction, a strong, deeply colored stock is obtained. Be careful to use only a little salt because the reduction can and will intensify the natural saltiness of the bones and trimmings.

MAKES ABOUT 1 QUART

2 to 2¼ pounds	finely chopped raw game bones and trimmings
⅓ cup	mirepoix (diced onion, carrot, celeriac, clove, and herbs)
4 to 5	juniper berries
4 cups	brown veal stock (see page 22)
6 cups	water
	Salt and freshly ground pepper

○ Roast the bones and trimmings in a roasting pan in a moderate oven until brown.

○ Remove any fat with a spoon or strain off, then add the mirepoix and juniper berries, and continue to roast carefully for a further 4 to 5 minutes.

○ Remove from the oven and transfer to a saucepan.

○ Add the brown veal stock and reduce to a glaze.

○ Add the water and simmer slowly for 1½ hours, occasionally skimming and removing the fat.

○ Strain through cheesecloth or a fine sieve and season to taste.

MEAT GLAZE
Glace de viande

Similar glazes can be made from fish, poultry, and game stocks.

MAKES ABOUT 1 CUP

5 quarts   brown veal stock (see page 22)

○ In your largest pan, simmer the stock until it has reduced considerably.

○ Pour reduced stock into a smaller pan and continue to simmer and reduce.

○ As the stock reduces, keep transferring into smaller saucepans. Keep the edges of the pan clean and clear with a flexible spatula.

○ Simmer until about 1 cup remains. Cool and store in the freezer. This quantity will be more than adequate for the relevant recipes in this book.

VEGETABLE STOCK
Fond de légumes

This vegetable stock is usually used for soups and vegetarian dishes. It can be used, reduced, in sauces like tomato and in salad dressings, instead of olive or other oil.

MAKES ABOUT 1 QUART

4 tablespoons	finely chopped onions
4 tablespoons	finely chopped leeks
2 tablespoons	finely chopped celery
3 tablespoons	finely chopped cabbage
2 tablespoons	finely chopped fennel
3 tablespoons	finely chopped tomatoes
6 cups	water
½	bay leaf
½	clove
	Salt and freshly ground pepper

○ Sweat the onions and leeks in a nonstick pan for 4 to 5 minutes.

○ Add the remaining vegetables and sweat for a further 10 minutes.

○ Add the water with the bay leaf and clove and simmer for 20 minutes.

○ Strain through cheesecloth or a fine sieve and season to taste.

FISH STOCK
Fond de poisson

To produce a good fish stock, only the bones of the freshest white fish
(sole, whiting, or turbot, for instance) should be used.

MAKES 5 CUPS

2 to 2¼ pounds	broken-up fish bones and trimmings
⅓ cup	white mirepoix (diced onions, white of leek, celeriac, and fennel leaves or dill)
¼ cup	mushroom trimmings
5 cups	water
	Salt and freshly ground pepper
	Lemon juice

○ Thoroughly wash the fish bones and trimmings.

○ Sweat the mirepoix and the mushroom trimmings in a nonstick pan for 4 to 5 minutes.

○ Transfer to a saucepan, add the fish bones, trimmings, and water, and simmer for 20 minutes, skimming occasionally.

○ Strain through cheesecloth or a fine sieve, allowing the stock to drip, and season with salt, pepper, and lemon juice.

COURT BOUILLON

This stock is used for poaching fish—salmon, turbot, sole—as well as for boiling lobster, shellfish, and the like.

MAKES ABOUT 2 QUARTS

2 quarts	water
½ pound	carrots, finely cut
⅔ cup	finely cut white of leek
⅔ cup	finely chopped onions
⅓ cup	finely cut celery
1	clove of garlic, unpeeled
5	parsley stems
1	small sprig of thyme
½	bay leaf
5	white peppercorns, crushed
3	coriander seeds
	Salt
4 tablespoons	white wine vinegar

○ Bring the water to the boil.

○ Add all the ingredients and allow to simmer for 10 minutes.

○ Strain through cheesecloth or a fine sieve, allowing stock to drip.

FROMAGE BLANC

TO MAKE EITHER 1½ CUPS OR 1 PINT

Low-fat ricotta cheese
Low-fat yogurt (see page 31)
A very small pinch of salt

○ Put the ricotta in the electric blender. For a 15-ounce (1½-cup) jar of ricotta, add 4 level tablespoons of yogurt. For a 1-pint jar (2 cups), add 5 level tablespoons plus 1 teaspoon of yogurt. Add the pinch of salt

○ Blend the mixture at high speed and taste several times. The objective is to purée the ricotta until there is no trace of graininess left in the texture. Keep blending until this happens. If you have trouble, the ricotta is not fresh enough; check the last sale date on the bottom of the jar when you buy it to be sure the date is a good month away. Store the fromage blanc, covered, in the refrigerator for 12 hours before using.

QUARK
Simple curd cheese

MAKES ABOUT 1⅓ CUPS

4½ cups   skim milk
Juice of ½ lemon

○ Bring the milk just to the boil, then add the lemon juice.

○ Remove pan from the heat and let cool for a while.

○ Bring to the boil again, then let the milk cool once more. It will have curdled.

○ Line a colander with cheesecloth and place over a deep pan or bowl (so that the colander is suspended and does not touch the bottom of the container).

○ Place the curdled milk in the cheesecloth and let the whey drain away.

○ Tie the corners of the cheesecloth tightly with string and hang up over the container to ensure that the whey drains away completely.

○ This takes approximately 1 hour. Do not press the cloth because this affects the flavor, and the quark will become sticky.

○ Take the quark out of the cheesecloth and put in the refrigerator to cool before use.

HOMEMADE YOGURT
Yogourt maison

Yogurt may be made in the following way or in a commercial yogurt-maker. Skim milk should be used in Cuisine Naturelle, as well as low-fat natural yogurt.
Keep a little yogurt as a starter for the next batch, but every few weeks use the commercial live variety, which has the right balance of culture. You can also make yogurt in the same way from goat's milk.

MAKES ABOUT 3½ CUPS

4½ cups	skim milk
1 tablespoon	low-fat natural yogurt

○ Bring the milk to the boil.

○ Cool to body temperature—98.6° F.

○ Put the yogurt into a wide-mouthed jar, pour the cooled milk over it, and whisk vigorously.

○ Cover the jar and put in a warm place overnight, or for a minimum of 6 hours, by which time it will have thickened into a delicious natural yogurt.

○ Cool in the refrigerator for a few hours before use.

○ Yogurt should never be overheated in cooking or it might curdle.

YOGURT CURD CHEESE

Curd cheese made from freshly made natural yogurt is very similar to quark and can be used in any recipe that specifies either curd cheese or quark. You can also make a curd cheese from freshly made goat's-milk yogurt.

MAKES ABOUT 2¼ CUPS

3½ cups   freshly made, low-fat natural yogurt
(see page 31)

○ Line a sieve or colander with cheesecloth and suspend over a deep bowl.

○ Put the yogurt into the sieve, cover, and leave for about 6 hours, or until all the whey has drained away.

○ Cool and use as soon as possible.

TOMATO CONCASSE
Tomates concassés

One of the basic sauces used in Cuisine Naturelle, tomato concassé has very few calories, is very light and colorful, and has a good flavor that goes well with both fish and meat.

SERVES 4

2 pounds	ripe tomatoes
2½ tablespoons	finely chopped shallot
	Whole clove of garlic, unpeeled
	A few sprigs of oregano and thyme
	Salt and freshly ground pepper

○ Remove the stems from the tomatoes and then blanch in hot water for approximately 12 seconds. Plunge into ice water and then peel.

○ Cut the peeled tomatoes in half, remove and discard the seeds, and chop into small pieces.

○ Sweat the shallot and whole clove of garlic well, without coloring, in a large nonstick pan.

○ Add the tomatoes and herbs and season with salt and pepper.

○ Cover and cook carefully for about 15 minutes until soft and all the liquid is evaporated.

○ Remove the garlic and herbs and, if necessary, season again with salt and pepper.

FILO DOUGH

This pastry—the only one used in Cuisine Naturelle recipes—is here made without oil or butter. It must be rolled extremely thin, and when baked it is crisp and light.

MAKES 1¼ TO 1½ POUNDS

2⅛ cups	white bread flour
¾ cup	cornstarch
½ teaspoon	salt
1⅛ cups	water

○ Sift the flour, cornstarch, and salt together into a bowl. Make a well in the center.

○ Put about half the water into the well and gradually draw the flour into the water, mixing smoothly and evenly. Add the remaining water and mix until dough is smooth and does not stick to the hands.

○ Cover dough with a damp cloth and let rest for 1 to 2 hours in a cool place. This allows it to develop its elasticity fully.

○ Cut the dough into quarters and cover the pieces not being rolled with a damp cloth. Start rolling out one piece, gradually making the sheet thinner and thinner. Use plenty of flour. It helps to warm the dough to make it pliable—cover with an inverted hot aluminum or stainless steel bowl.

○ If the dough sheet becomes too large and unwieldy, cut in half and continue to roll. Then, when the dough is as thin as possible by rolling, place sheet over the back of the hand and pull gently down from the edges to stretch even more. Work carefully so that it does not break.

○ Roll other pieces of dough in the same way and cover dough and sheets at all times with a damp cloth. Use sheets as quickly as possible.

RAVIOLI DOUGH
Pâte à ravioli

This dough can also be used as the basis for Chinese-type dumplings—
for soup—and for tortellini.

SERVES 4

¾ cup, less 1 tablespoon,	all-purpose flour, sifted
Scant ¼ cup	semolina
½	egg
	Pinch of salt
¼ cup	water

○ Mix the flour and semolina together, then make a well in the center.

○ Place the egg, salt, and water in the well.

○ Gradually mix the flour in toward the middle.

○ Knead the mixture to a smooth, firm dough, then let rest for 1 to 2 hours before use.

HERB MIXTURES
Mélanges des herbes

The blending of herbs warms the spirit and delights the senses of taste and smell. Their flavor should never dominate a dish or product but should create a harmony.

These herb mixtures have been created to cut down on the use of salt. The proportions have been very carefully worked out so that the flavors of the herbs do not overpower the dish in which they are used.

For fish and shellfish:

2 teaspoons	dill, finely cut
1 teaspoon	thyme, finely chopped
1 teaspoon	basil, finely cut
1 teaspoon	chervil, plucked apart with the fingers
½ teaspoon	coriander, leaves pulled off stems and plucked apart with the fingers
½ teaspoon	tarragon, finely snipped with scissors

For meat and poultry:

2 teaspoons	thyme	
1½ teaspoons	marjoram	} finely chopped
1 teaspoon	rosemary	
½ teaspoon	oregano	
1 teaspoon	basil	} finely cut
¼ teaspoon	sage	

For game:

2 teaspoons	rosemary	
1 teaspoon	savory	} finely chopped
1 teaspoon	thyme	
½ teaspoon	juniper berries, crushed	
½ teaspoon	tarragon, finely snipped with scissors	

For vegetables:

1 teaspoon	oregano, finely chopped
1 teaspoon	dill, finely cut
1 teaspoon	chervil, plucked apart with fingers
1 teaspoon	borage, finely cut

○ Use only fresh herbs; cut, snip, and chop as specified; and mix together. Use a pinch or as much as desired in individual recipes, and you will find that the need for salt is reduced by at least 50 percent.

○ Fresh herbs are best, of course, but the mixtures can be made up and kept in the freezer in small containers.

○ Chopped garlic can be added to the mixtures if desired, but in small quantity only because it can be overpowering (and it should never be frozen).

APPETIZERS

An appetizer is the prelude to the high point of a meal, usually a main course of meat or fish. Served before the meat, the appetizer should, however, offer a clear contrast to the succeeding courses. It is meant to excite the palate but not appease hunger, so it must be light; it is the introduction to the meal, so it should be interesting in conception as well as exciting for the eye—for beauty of ingredients, color, and arrangement on the plate are all major contributors to the enjoyment of a dish or meal.

The recipes in this section have been designed especially to fulfill all the foregoing requirements, as well as to follow the basics of Cuisine Naturelle. It is commonly acknowledged these days that people are eating considerably less—which is desirable for good health—and none of the following recipes contains the ingredients that are excluded from Cuisine Naturelle—butter, oils, cream, or alcohol. Many of the appetizers could be eaten as a light main course or expanded to serve as a main course; indeed, two appetizers could be served *instead* of a main course. Thus this section is the longest in the book.

The majority of recipes consist of a colorful, decorative, and healthful salad base with a little added meat or fish protein—the ideal prelude to a light meal. Here also are thin slices of meat or fish to excite the palate, vegetable and fish terrines, as well as many ideas for light and attractive pasta appetizers.

To cut down on salt, one of the herb mixtures (see page 36) could be used instead of some salt in any of the recipes.

CRAB SALAD WITH COCONUT
Salade de crabe à ma façon

For a perfect presentation, saw two coconuts in half and saw off a slice
at the bottom of each half so that it will stand properly.

SERVES 4

8 ounces	white crab meat
1 tablespoon	finely chopped shallots
1	tomato, peeled, seeded, and cut into thin julienne strips
1	stalk of celery, trimmed and cut into thin julienne strips
2 ounces	slender green beans, trimmed and blanched
1 ounce	shredded fresh coconut
	Juice of ½ lemon
1 tablespoon	red wine vinegar
	Salt and freshly ground pepper
1	heart of lettuce (bibb or boston)
1	head of radicchio
2	endives
2	pink grapefruit
1	orange
1 tablespoon	freshly cut chives

○ Mix together the crab meat, shallots, tomato and celery julienne, green beans, and coconut.

○ Moisten with lemon juice and vinegar and season to taste with salt and pepper.

○ Wash and dry the salad leaves.

○ Cut away the peel and white pith from the grapefruit and orange and carefully remove all the separate segments of fruit.

○ Arrange the salad leaves in four halved coconut shells (or on plates).

○ Spoon the crab mixture on top and garnish with the grapefruit and orange segments. Sprinkle with chives and serve at once.

SQUID SALAD
WITH MUSTARD AND HERB DRESSING
Salade de calamares à la sauce moutarde et aux herbes

SERVES 4

6   squid, about 4½ inches in body length
     Salt and freshly ground pepper
     Juice of ½ lemon
2   endives, separated, cut into leaves, washed, and dried
1   small head of lettuce, prepared, washed, and dried
1   medium tomato, peeled, seeded, and cut into strips

Mustard and herb dressing:

¼ cup   quark (see page 30)
4 teaspoons   tarragon vinegar
2 teaspoons   soy sauce
1 teaspoon   herb mustard
2 teaspoons   cut fresh herbs (such as chervil, chives, parsley, basil)
2 tablespoons   vegetable stock (see page 26)
     Salt and freshly ground pepper

○ Take the squid by the tentacles, pull off the heads, and remove the insides and spines.

○ Cut off the tentacles below the eyes and put to one side.

○ Loosen the gristle from inside the squid and pull out.

○ Remove the ink sacs and any fluid. (Save the ink for making black noodles or squid sauce.)

○ Wash the body and tentacles well and place on paper towels.

○ Chop the tentacles and peel the outer skin from the body.

○ Slice the meat into small pieces. Season with salt, pepper, and lemon juice.

○ For the dressing, mix all the ingredients together in a blender or food processor, or with a whisk, and season to taste with salt and pepper.

○ Sauté the squid very quickly in a nonstick pan until opaque.

○ Put some mustard and herb dressing on a plate and place the sautéed squid pieces on top. Toss the salad ingredients in a little dressing and arrange on the side of the plate.

WHITE AND GREEN ASPARAGUS
SALAD WITH SCALLOPS
Méli-mélo d'asperges et coquilles St. Jacques

SERVES 4

6	medium spears of white asparagus, trimmed and peeled
16	small spears of green asparagus, trimmed and peeled
12	large sea scallops
1	baby carrot, peeled
4 tablespoons	low-fat natural yogurt (see page 31)
	Juice of ½ lemon
	Salt and freshly ground pepper
1	heart of romaine lettuce, washed and dried
1	heart of oak leaf lettuce, washed and dried
	A few leaves of chicory
	Fresh chervil to garnish

○ Cook the asparagus in salted water for 2 to 3 minutes until just tender. Drain, then cool quickly in ice-cold water. Drain again and keep on a damp cloth. Cut white asparagus in half lengthwise.

○ Wash the scallops well, then cut in half.

○ Make channels down the length of the carrot with a cannelle knife, then slice the carrot thinly. Blanch slices in boiling water for 1 minute. Drain, then cool in ice water. Drain.

○ Mix together the yogurt and lemon juice. Season with salt and pepper.

○ Arrange the salad leaves, asparagus, and carrots on individual plates. Spoon a little yogurt onto each plate.

○ Sauté the scallops in a nonstick pan for 15 seconds. Season to taste with salt and pepper and arrange on top of the salad.

○ Garnish with tiny sprigs of chervil.

SPINACH SALAD
WITH STILTON SAUCE
Feuilles d'épinards en salade au Stilton

Fresh raw spinach is delicious, but tender lettuce, chicory, or radicchio
may be used instead.

SERVES 4

1	red pepper
	About ½ pound tender spinach leaves, thick stems removed
3	slices bread
1	clove of garlic, peeled and crushed
2 teaspoons	lemon juice
1 teaspoon	strong mustard
⅞ cup	low-fat natural yogurt (see page 31)
1½ ounces	Stilton cheese
	Salt and freshly ground pepper
¼ cup	chopped parsley
2 teaspoons	cut basil

○ Bake the pepper in the oven at a high temperature, turning occasionally, until dark spots appear on the skin.

○ Remove from the oven and cover for 3 to 4 minutes with a damp cloth. Remove the skin, cut pepper in half, take out the core and seeds, and cut the flesh into fine strips.

○ Wash the spinach well, drain, and dry well on a towel.

○ Cut the bread into small cubes and bake in the oven at 400° F for about 10 minutes until golden. Add the crushed garlic and mix well to flavor all the cubes.

○ Mix the lemon juice, mustard, and yogurt together well. Crush the Stilton with a fork and mix into the yogurt. Season to taste.

○ Put the spinach leaves and red pepper strips into a bowl. Pour the sauce over them and mix in well.

○ Sprinkle with parsley, basil, and garlic croutons. Serve immediately, or the tender spinach will quickly fall apart.

CHICORY WITH SMOKED HAM
AND WALNUT SALAD
Salade de chicorée au jambon fumé et aux noix

SERVES 4

4 ounces	shelled walnuts
4 ounces	lean smoked ham, cut into thin strips
1	small head of iceberg lettuce
½	head of chicory
1	red onion, cut in fine slices, or 3 to 4 scallions, sliced
1½ teaspoons	honey
4 tablespoons	white vinegar
	Salt and freshly ground pepper

○ Place the walnuts on a baking sheet in the oven at 350° F for about 10 minutes until golden. Allow to cool slightly, then rub off as much skin as possible. Roughly chop the nuts.

○ Sauté the ham in a nonstick pan until crisp. Remove from the pan and reserve any meat juices in the pan.

○ Wash and dry the lettuce and chicory and tear into bite-sized pieces. Place in a large bowl with the nuts, ham, and sliced onion.

○ Add the honey to the pan and heat until dissolved. Add the vinegar and bring to a boil. Pour immediately over the salad and toss well.

○ Season with salt and pepper and serve at once.

RAW MUSHROOM SALAD
Salade de champignons crus

Mushrooms are a perfect Cuisine Naturelle vegetable, containing no sugar or starch. Here, served raw, they retain their full nutritional value.

SERVES 4

½ cup	buttermilk or freshly soured skim milk
½ cup	fromage blanc (see page 29)
1 tablespoon	lemon juice
1	small onion, peeled and finely chopped
2 tablespoons	freshly chopped parsley
	Pinch of salt and freshly ground pepper
½ pound	button mushrooms, washed and trimmed
1	heart of bibb lettuce, washed and dried
1	tomato, cut into 8 wedges
1 tablespoon	freshly cut chives

○ Mix together the buttermilk, fromage blanc, lemon juice, onion, and parsley until as smooth as possible. Season to taste with a little salt and pepper.

○ Thinly slice the mushrooms and carefully mix into the sauce. Cover and leave to marinate for 30 minutes.

○ Mix well to coat the mushroom slices evenly, then drain.

○ Arrange the lettuce leaves and mushroom salad on each of four plates. Garnish with the tomato wedges and chives.

NETTLE SALAD WITH GREEN TOMATOES AND SORREL
Salade d'orties aux tomates vertes et oseille

Gather the nettle leaves (and tops too) with gloves. Because sorrel contains oxalic acid, only one leaf per person is used, but its sour and refreshing taste is a delicious addition to any salad. To vary the recipe, ¼ pound finely sliced prosciutto can be mixed with the dressing and added to the salad.

SERVES 4

¼ pound	tender young nettle leaves
⅛ pound	dandelion leaves
	A few dandelion flowers
4	sorrel leaves

Dressing:

6 tablespoons	strong vegetable stock (see page 26)
3 tablespoons	wine vinegar
	Salt and freshly ground pepper
4	green tomatoes, peeled, seeded, and diced

○ Wash the nettles, dandelion leaves and flowers, and sorrel.

○ Finely shred the sorrel and mix together with the nettles and dandelions.

○ For the dressing, whisk together the stock, vinegar, salt, and pepper. Add the tomatoes.

○ Warm the dressing gently in a bowl over a pan of simmering water.

○ Pour the dressing over the salad, mix carefully, and serve immediately.

SALAD WITH GREEN BEANS
AND SWEETBREADS
Mélange de salades aux ris de veau

SERVES 4

About ½ pound	calf's sweetbreads (½ pair)
1	onion, chopped
1	carrot, chopped
1	leek, chopped
1	stalk of celery, chopped
10	black peppercorns, crushed
3	juniper berries
1	bay leaf
5 ounces	green beans
4 tablespoons	reduced white veal stock (see page 20)
2 tablespoons	wine vinegar
2	small shallots, finely chopped
	Salt and freshly ground pepper
½	head of chicory
½	head of oak leaf lettuce
½	bunch of watercress
2	medium tomatoes, seeded and diced
	A few sprigs of flat-leafed parsley, cut into julienne

○ Wash the sweetbreads, then leave to soak for 2 hours, changing the water frequently.

○ Cook in lightly salted water with the onion, carrot, leek, celery, peppercorns, juniper berries, and bay leaf for about 30 minutes until tender. Drain and remove membrane from sweetbreads. Discard vegetables.

○ Trim and cut the green beans diagonally into 1-inch lengths. Blanch in boiling salted water for about 1 minute. Refresh in ice-cold water. Drain.

○ Make a dressing with the reduced stock, vinegar, shallots, and seasoning.

○ Slice the sweetbreads and marinate in half the dressing for about 8 to 10 minutes. Wash the salad leaves and toss in remaining dressing.

○ Arrange salad leaves and beans on four individual plates and place the sweetbreads on top.

○ Garnish with tomato dice and julienne of parsley.

QUAIL AND ARTICHOKE SALAD WITH NUTS
Salade d'artichauts et cailles aux noix

SERVES 4

4	globe artichokes
4 tablespoons	strong vegetable stock (see page 26)
2 tablespoons	wine vinegar
	Salt and freshly ground pepper
4	quail
1	head of oak leaf lettuce, washed and dried
4	leaves of lamb's lettuce (corn salad), washed and dried
4	walnut halves, skinned and chopped

Sauce:

3 tablespoons	*each* of diced onion, leek, and carrot
3	juniper berries
1	sprig of thyme
¼	bay leaf
1	tomato, diced
2 cups	water

○ Break off the stalks of the artichokes close to the base. Wash artichokes well, then cook in boiling salted water with a dash of vinegar or lemon juice. Cool, remove the leaves, and choke and trim the hearts.

○ Mix the stock and vinegar together with salt and pepper to taste.

○ Cut the artichoke hearts into thin slices and marinate in about half this dressing.

○ Remove the breasts from the quail and reserve the legs and carcass for the sauce.

○ To make the sauce, sauté the quail trimmings in a nonstick pan until well browned on all sides. Add the vegetables and herbs and continue to sauté for a few minutes. Add water and simmer for about 30 minutes.

○ Strain sauce through a fine cloth and return to a clean pan. Bring to a boil and boil until reduced by half.

○ Sauté the quail breasts in a nonstick pan for 1 minute on each side, or until they are still just pink.

○ Arrange the salad leaves, artichoke slices, and walnuts on the individual plates. Spoon over the dressing.

○ Arrange the quail breasts on top and glaze with sauce. Serve at once.

WARM CHICKEN LIVER SALAD WITH YOGURT DRESSING
Salade de foie de volaille tiède, sauce au yogourt

The fresh yeast makes this dressing light and foamy and gives it a
pleasant, nutty flavor.

SERVES 4

½ pound	dandelion leaves or 1 head of chicory, well washed and torn
4	tomatoes, peeled and seeded
7 ounces	chicken livers, trimmed, large ones cut in half
	Salt and freshly ground pepper
2 tablespoons	freshly cut chives

Yogurt dressing:

4 ounces	low-fat natural yogurt (see page 31)
2 teaspoons	wine vinegar
2 teaspoons	soy sauce
1 teaspoon	brewer's yeast
2 teaspoons	cut mixed fresh herbs (such as parsley, dill, basil)
2 teaspoons	finely chopped onion
1	sliver of garlic, crushed
½ teaspoon	English (strong) mustard
	Salt and freshly ground pepper

○ Arrange the salad leaves on four individual plates.

○ Cut the tomatoes into julienne strips.

○ Season the chicken livers and sauté in a nonstick pan until lightly browned on all sides but still pink in the center.

○ Arrange livers on the salad leaves and sprinkle with tomato julienne and chives.

○ For the dressing, mix all the ingredients together until evenly blended and season to taste.

○ Serve the salad at once, with the yogurt dressing passed separately.

COTTAGE GARDEN SALAD
Salade du jardin

A basic—and delicious—salad, which can be served as an appetizer or
an accompanying salad to a main dish.

SERVES 4

1	small head of lettuce
1	small head of radicchio
¼ pound	spinach leaves, tough stems removed
1	bunch of watercress, stems removed
¼ pound	raw mushrooms, thinly sliced
2	carrots, peeled and thinly sliced
6	radishes, thinly sliced
1 tablespoon	chives, finely cut

Dressing:

1	red pepper, cored, seeded, and chopped
⅔ cup	skim milk
3 tablespoons	chopped onion
1	medium tomato, peeled and finely chopped
1 teaspoon	Dijon-style mustard
	A pinch of paprika
	Salt and freshly ground pepper

○ Wash and dry the salad and spinach leaves. Tear into bite-sized pieces and mix with the washed watercress leaves.

○ Combine the mushroom, carrot, and radish slices with the salad leaves. Sprinkle with chives.

○ For the dressing, steam the red pepper pieces for 3 to 4 minutes until just tender. Cool, then purée with the remaining ingredients in a blender or food processor until well mixed. Season to taste with salt and pepper.

○ Mix dressing into the salad leaves just before serving.

THIN SLICES OF HALIBUT
WITH VEGETABLES
Émincé de flétan oriental

The halibut is to be eaten simply marinated, so it must be of top quality
and very fresh.

SERVES 4

1 pound	halibut, skinned
	Juice of 1 lemon
	Salt and freshly ground pepper
2 tablespoons	Meaux mustard
2 tablespoons	Dijon mustard
2 tablespoons	rice vinegar
4 tablespoons	fish stock (see page 27)
⅛ pound	daikon (white radish) ⎫
	About 6 red radishes ⎪
1	medium carrot ⎬ cut into juliene strips
½	stalk of celery ⎪
1 ounce	enoki mushrooms ⎭
2 to 3 tablespoons	slivered almonds, toasted
4	small bunches of lamb's lettuce

○ Slice the halibut very thinly and season with lemon juice, salt, and pepper.

○ Let marinate for 5 to 10 minutes in a cool place.

○ Meanwhile, mix the two mustards, vinegar, and fish stock together. Season well and let stand at room temperature. Mix again before serving.

○ Spoon the mustard sauce over the fish.

○ Garnish with the julienne of vegetables, mushrooms, slivered almonds, and lamb's lettuce.

MARINATED SALMON
Saumon mariné

Here are two methods of "pickling" salmon: one which takes 24 hours and one which takes only 10 to 15 minutes. In both cases the salmon is to be served raw, so it must be extremely fresh. In the first recipe, the amount of sugar has been reduced to a minimum.

Version 1: SERVES 8

1	whole salmon, about 3 to 3½ pounds
1⅔ tablespoons	salt
1 heaping tablespoon	sugar
½ cup	freshly cut dill
1 tablespoon	white peppercorns, coarsely ground
8	small bunches of dill to garnish

○ Carefully fillet the salmon and remove the bones.

○ Coat with a mixture of the remaining ingredients other than the garnish. Place in a suitable dish, cover, and store in the refrigerator.

○ Marinate the fish for 24 hours, occasionally moistening it with the liquid that is produced.

○ Remove from the marinade and cut as smoked salmon. Garnish with the dill.

Version 2: SERVES 4

14 ounces	fillet of salmon (after skinning and trimming well)
	Juice of 2 limes
1 tablespoon	each of freshly cut chives, chervil, and finely snipped tarragon
1 tablespoon	Meaux mustard
	Salt and freshly ground pepper
2	small lemons to garnish

○ Cut the salmon into very thin slices and arrange on a suitable dish.

○ Whisk together the remaining ingredients (except lemons) and pour over the salmon. Let marinate for 10 minutes.

○ Garnish simply with lemon halves. If serving as a main course, an ideal accompaniment is the Raw Mushroom Salad (see page 47).

MARINATED SALMON
WITH POACHED EGGS
Saumon mariné aux oeufs pochés

The first version of the previous recipe is more suitable for this dish.
The sauce is not vital, but it adds a piquant flavor.

SERVES 4

4	medium eggs
	Water for poaching, with a dash of vinegar added
12	thin slices of marinated salmon
2 teaspoons	lemon juice
8	lettuce leaves, well washed and dried
	Salt, freshly ground pepper, and paprika
	A little dill for garnish

Sauce:

⅔ cup	fromage blanc (see page 29)
1½ teaspoons	mild French mustard
2 tablespoons	liquid from the marinade, strained
	Cayenne, salt, and freshly ground pepper
	A little fresh dill

○ Poach the eggs carefully in the vinegar water for about 5 minutes.

○ Remove with a skimming ladle and cool in cold water.

○ Place on a cloth and trim with a knife or scissors.

○ Arrange three thin slices of salmon in the center of each plate and sprinkle with lemon juice.

○ Arrange two lettuce leaves attractively on top of the salmon.

○ Season with salt and pepper.

○ Place an egg in the center of each circle of lettuce and garnish with the paprika and dill.

○ Mix all the sauce ingredients together well and serve separately.

SALMON TERRINE WITH VEGETABLES
Terrine de saumon fantaisie

It is not necessary to serve a sauce with this terrine, although one is
included in the recipe.

SERVES 14

2 pounds	fillet of salmon, skinned and cut into thin *escalopes*
2½ cups	fish stock (see page 27)
2 tablespoons	white herb vinegar
	Juice of ½ lemon
	About ½ pound broccoli, cut into tiny florets, and stalks diced
¾ pound	spinach, washed and thick stems removed
½ pound	carrots, peeled and cooked until just tender
6	tomatoes, peeled, seeded, and diced
1 ounce	gelatin
	Fresh chives and carrot leaves or dill to garnish

Sauce:

Scant 2 cups	low-fat natural yogurt (see page 31)
1 tablespoon	English (strong) mustard
2 tablespoons	freshly cut dill
	Salt and freshly ground pepper

○ Lightly poach the salmon *escalopes* in the stock, with the vinegar and lemon juice, for 1 to 2 minutes. Drain and cool. Strain the stock and reserve.

○ Blanch the broccoli in boiling salted water. Drain and cool in ice water.

○ Blanch the spinach and cool as above.

○ Cut the carrots into strips lengthwise.

○ Arrange alternate layers of salmon and vegetables, including the tomato dice, in a 1½-quart terrine.

○ Dissolve the gelatin in about one-quarter of the fish stock over gentle heat. Add remaining stock. Chill until the consistency of unbeaten egg white, then pour into the terrine. Chill until set.

○ To make the sauce, mix all the ingredients together, then chill.

○ Serve the terrine in slices, garnished with herbs. Pass the sauce separately.

TURBOT TARTARE WITH TOFU
Tartare de turbot au tofu

The fish is marinated in lemon juice, not cooked, so make sure that it is of the best quality and as fresh as possible. The tomatoes can be served as a canapé as well as an appetizer.

SERVES 4

½ pound	fillet of turbot
4 tablespoons	lemon juice
⅓ cup	finely chopped shallots
1 tablespoon	chopped parsley
1	radish, peeled and finely grated
1 ounce	tofu
	Pinch of cayenne
	Salt and freshly ground pepper
8	medium tomatoes
1	large cucumber
	Cut dill

○ Remove any bones from the fish and then chop the flesh very finely. Place in a bowl with 3 tablespoons of the lemon juice. Leave for about 30 minutes.

○ Mix together the shallots, parsley, and radish.

○ Beat together the remaining lemon juice and the tofu. Add the shallot mixture.

○ Check the fish to see that it is opaque all the way through, then drain and mix with the shallot and tofu mixture. Season to taste with cayenne, salt, and pepper.

○ Remove the "lids" from the tomatoes and scoop out the seeds. Sprinkle with salt and pepper. Cut a piece from the base of each so that they will stand properly.

○ Drain excess liquid from the turbot. Pipe or spoon turbot into the tomatoes, then arrange on individual plates.

○ Cut the cucumber into julienne strips and spoon around the filled tomatoes. Sprinkle with cut dill and serve with small pieces of whole wheat toast.

LEEK TART WITH MOZZARELLA AND APPLES
Tarte de poireaux au mozzarella et aux pommes fruits

Other relatively low-fat cheeses can be used instead of mozzarella—
raclette and Edam, for instance.

SERVES 8

1 pound	young leeks, washed well and cut into ½-inch slices
	Salt and freshly ground pepper
8	basil leaves, cut into fine strips
½ pound	potatoes, washed, peeled, and cut into slices, ¼ inch thick
7 ounces	filo dough, rolled out thinly (see page 34)
6 ounces	mozzarella cheese, diced
1	cooking apple, peeled, cored, and cut into small pieces

○ Heat a nonstick pan and sauté the leek slices for about 10 minutes, turning constantly, until they are soft.

○ Season with salt, pepper, and basil.

○ Cook the potato slices in a little water until just soft, about 7 to 8 minutes. Allow to cool.

○ Divide the very thin filo dough into four squares, about 12 × 12 inches.

○ Place three pieces of filo on a nonstick baking sheet. Arrange alternate layers of potato and leek on top.

○ Sprinkle with the mozzarella dice and then the pieces of apple.

○ Top with remaining sheet of filo and seal edges. Prick several times with a fork and bake slowly in the oven at 325° F for about 30 minutes.

○ The tart should be baked very slowly. If the top starts to brown too quickly, reduce the heat or cover loosely with foil. Serve it warm.

STUFFED ZUCCHINI FLOWERS
WITH RED PEPPER SAUCE
Fleurs de courgettes farcies à la sauce de piments doux

SERVES 4

5 ounces	fillet of pike (or other white fish), skinned and boned
1	egg white
	Salt and freshly ground pepper
5 ounces	fromage blanc (see page 29)
4	zucchini with their flowers
⅞ cup	fish stock (see page 27)

Red pepper sauce:

2	medium red peppers
1 tablespoon	finely chopped shallots
1	small clove of garlic, peeled and chopped
	A few sprigs of fresh thyme
1¾ cups	fish stock (see page 27)
	A pinch of sugar
	Salt and freshly ground pepper

○ To make the sauce, wash and trim the peppers and cut into large pieces. Sweat the shallots and garlic in a nonstick pan over gentle heat, without browning. Add the red peppers and thyme.

○ Add the fish stock and simmer, uncovered, for about 20 minutes until the peppers are tender. Process in a blender or food processor and season to taste with sugar, salt, and pepper.

○ Purée the pike fillet in a food processor until smooth. Add the egg white and a pinch of salt and pepper and purée again until well mixed. Transfer the mixture to a bowl.

○ Beat in the fromage blanc, a little at a time, with a wooden spoon. Season to taste.

○ Place the bowl in a larger bowl of ice for about 15 minutes.

○ Meanwhile, wash and dry the zucchini very carefully.

○ Place the chilled pike mousse in a pastry bag (or use a teaspoon) and carefully fill the zucchini flowers.

○ Make even cuts in the zucchini almost to the flower.

○ Steam the zucchini over the fish stock for 3 to 4 minutes.

○ Spoon a little warm red pepper sauce onto each of four plates, place the zucchini on top, and serve at once.

CRAB CRESCENTS DORCHESTER
Croissants de crabe Dorchester

SERVES 4

3 tablespoons	finely chopped shallots
11 ounces	white crab meat, without shell
½	clove of garlic, peeled and crushed
1 teaspoon	freshly cut basil
	Salt and freshly ground pepper
1	recipe of ravioli dough (see page 35)
1	egg, beaten lightly
⅞ cup	tomato coulis (see page 141)
4 tablespoons	freshly grated Parmesan cheese
12	basil leaves to garnish

○ Sweat the shallots carefully in a nonstick pan without browning.

○ Add the crab meat and stir well.

○ Add the garlic, cut basil, and salt and pepper to taste. Let it cool.

○ Roll out the ravioli dough very thinly on a lightly floured surface to a rectangle about 6 × 9 inches. Cut out twenty-four squares about 1½ × 1½ inches each, then cut each square into two triangles.

○ Brush the edge of each triangle with beaten egg.

○ Place a small amount of filling on each triangle and roll up, from the longest edge, bringing the ends round to make a crescent shape. Press lightly to enclose filling.

○ Cook the crescents in boiling salted water for 4 to 5 minutes. Drain well.

○ Mix with hot tomato coulis, then arrange on a suitable dish and sprinkle with grated Parmesan.

○ Brown under the grill, then serve immediately, garnished with fresh basil leaves.

CRAB TERRINE
WITH AVOCADO SAUCE
Terrine de crabe, sauce aux avocats

SERVES 15

7 ounces	smoked salmon, sliced thinly
4	eggs
2 cups	quark (see page 30)
1 pound	cooked white crab meat (carefully checked to remove any small pieces of shell)
1	medium cucumber
¾ pound	tomatoes, peeled, seeded, and cut into small dice
2 tablespoons	freshly cut chives
	Freshly ground pepper
15	cherry tomatoes

Avocado sauce:

2	medium, ripe avocadoes
	Juice of ½ lemon
⅝ cup	low-fat natural yogurt (see page 31)
	Salt and freshly ground pepper

○ Line 1½-quart terrine with slices of smoked salmon, leaving a little to cover the top.

○ Whisk the eggs and mix in the quark and crab meat.

○ Cut the cucumber into four lengthwise and remove the seeds. Cut into small dice.

○ Add cucumber, tomatoes, and chives to the crab mixture. Season with pepper only.

○ Transfer the mixture to the salmon-lined terrine, fold over any pieces of smoked salmon, and top with the reserved slices. Cover with foil.

○ Poach in a bain-marie (or a roasting pan filled with hot water) in the oven at 325° F for about 1¼ to 1½ hours until a skewer comes out clean and warm if pressed into the center.

○ Remove from the bain-marie and allow to cool, then turn out onto a suitable dish.

○ To make the sauce, peel the avocadoes and remove the pits. Push through a sieve, then mix in the remaining ingredients. Season to taste.

○ To serve, remove the tops from the cherry tomatoes, scoop out the seeds, and fill with a little avocado sauce. Arrange a slice of terrine on each plate and garnish with a tomato and a little extra sauce.

WILD MUSHROOM TERRINE
WITH CHIVES
Terrine de champignons sauvages à la ciboulette

In the picture opposite we have used a mushroom-shaped mold, but any terrine dish can be used—if less wittily! Any mushrooms can be used if some of those below are not available.

SERVES 15

5 ounces	chanterelles (girolles)
5 ounces	oyster mushrooms (pleurotes), sliced
5 ounces	cèpes, sliced
5 ounces	button mushrooms, sliced
4 ounces	horn of plenty mushrooms (trompettes)
4 ounces	St. George's mushrooms (mousserons)
	Salt and freshly ground pepper
1 ounce	gelatin
2¼ cups	white poultry stock (see page 19)
	Freshly cut chives
1⅜ cups	fromage blanc (see page 29)
	Paprika
	Fresh chives to garnish

○ Trim and clean the mushrooms, then wash and dry well. Sauté in a nonstick frying pan over high heat, then allow to cool. Season to taste with salt and pepper.

○ Dissolve the gelatin in about one-quarter of the warm stock, then add the remaining stock.

○ Chill the stock until the consistency of unbeaten egg white.

○ Stir in the mushrooms and cut chives and transfer to a 1½-quart terrine dish.

○ Cover and chill until set.

○ To serve, cut into slices and arrange each slice on a plate with a small quenelle of seasoned fromage blanc sprinkled with paprika and a few short lengths of fresh chives.

MARINATED FILLET OF BEEF JAPANESE STYLE
Filet de boeuf mariné à la japonaise

These paper-thin, raw beef slices are served with leeks in a dressing that needs no further salt because of the salt in the soy sauce.

SERVES 4

½ pound	fillet of beef without fat
	Juice of 1 lemon
	Salt and freshly ground pepper
2	large leeks, white part only, cut into 2-inch lengths
3 ounces	oyster mushrooms
¼ pound	chicory and oak leaf lettuce, washed and dried well

Dressing:

2 tablespoons	sherry vinegar
2 tablespoons	white wine vinegar
6 tablespoons	soy sauce
	Freshly ground pepper

○ Cut the beef fillet into thin slices and, layering it between sheets of plastic film, carefully beat until extremely thin.

○ Sprinkle the meat with about half the lemon juice and some salt and pepper.

○ Cook the leeks with remaining lemon juice and some salt in boiling water until just tender, then drain.

○ Mix together the dressing ingredients, then marinate the leeks while still warm.

○ Season the oyster mushrooms with salt and pepper and sauté them quickly until brown in a nonstick pan.

○ Arrange the salad leaves and the leeks on individual serving plates and carefully arrange the thin meat slices on top.

○ Garnish with the still-warm oyster mushrooms and serve immediately.

MOSAIC OF SEASONAL VEGETABLES
Mosaïque de légumes à ma façon

It is vital for this recipe to blanch the vegetables to the *al dente* stage only. They must still be crunchy to keep their flavor and texture during the later poaching process. To retain maximum flavor, cool them quickly in their own stock surrounded by ice or in some cold vegetable stock over ice. Different vegetables can be used according to season, but they should all be chosen for color and texture, so that they contribute to the attractiveness of the finished dish.

SERVES 15

4	globe artichokes
	Salt
	Juice of 1½ lemons
3	bunches of watercress, well washed and stems removed
4	eggs, beaten
2 cups	fromage blanc (see page 29)
½ pound	small carrots, peeled, blanched, and cut in quarters lengthwise
About 1 pound	broccoli, cleaned, blanched, and divided into florets
¼ pound	snowpeas, trimmed and blanched
¼ pound	tiny green beans, trimmed and blanched
About ½ pound	small zucchini, blanched and cut in quarters lengthwise
11 ounces	chanterelles (or any other mushroom)

○ Break off the stems of the artichokes and cut away three-quarters of the leafy head.

○ Remove the remaining leaves from the artichoke bottoms and scrape out the choke.

○ Blanch the bottoms in boiling salted water with the juice of 1 lemon for 3 minutes. Drain and place in fresh boiling salted water with the remaining lemon juice. Cook until just tender, about 10 to 12 minutes.

○ Allow to cool in the water, sitting in a bowl of ice. Slice the artichoke bottoms.

○ Blanch the watercress in boiling salted water. Drain, cool, then purée until smooth.

○ Mix the eggs with the fromage blanc.

○ Stir the puréed watercress into one-third of the cheese mixture.

○ Line the base of a 1½-quart terrine dish with parchment or wax paper. Spoon the watercress mixture into the terrine and level the surface.

○ Arrange the carrots on top in an even layer.

○ Continue layering the vegetables with a thin layer of plain cheese mixture between each vegetable layer.

○ Cover with foil and poach in a bain-marie (or roasting pan filled with hot water) at 325° F for about 1 hour until a skewer pressed into the center comes out clean and warm.

○ Remove from the bain-marie, cool, and then chill until required. Serve in slices. Because it is quite moist, the terrine does not require a sauce.

STEAMED RED MULLET FILLETS WITH VEGETABLES
Rouget à la vapeur et aux légumes

SERVES 4

4	red mullet, about 6 ounces each, filleted and boned*
	Salt and freshly ground pepper
1	carrot, peeled
2	small white onions
1 tablespoon	lemon juice
1 tablespoon	white wine vinegar
2 tablespoons	reduced fish stock (see page 27)
16	pieces of fresh chives, cut into 2-inch strips

○ Season the fish fillets with salt and pepper and place skin side up on parchment paper.

○ Cut the carrot with a cannelle knife, then slice into paper-thin rounds.

○ Cut the onions into thin rings.

○ Blanch the carrot and onion in boiling water until just tender, about 1 to 2 minutes.

○ Sprinkle fish fillets with the carrot and onion and steam for 3 to 5 minutes.

○ Heat the lemon juice and vinegar. Whisk in the stock; season with salt and pepper.

○ Arrange the fish fillets on a plate, spoon over the sauce, and garnish with cut chives.

*If mullet is unavailable, trout or red snapper are good substitutes.

OYSTER SAUSAGES
WITH SAFFRON AND INK SAUCES
Saucisses des huîtres "jaune et noir"

This dish was created for a gathering of eighteen chefs voted the world's best in a recent book. It took place in the Dorchester's Terrace Restaurant and, not unnaturally, I was trying to create something very unusual, with exciting flavors, colors, and textures.

SERVES 4

7 ounces	salmon trout, skinned and boned
4 ounces	tofu
	Salt and freshly ground pepper
24	oysters
2 teaspoons	finely cut dill
	Juice of ½ lemon
16 to 20 inches	sausage casings, soaked in water

Saffron sauce:

1¾ cups	fish stock (see page 27)
3½ tablespoons	finely chopped shallots
	A few strands of saffron
½ cup	fromage blanc (see page 29)
	Salt and freshly ground pepper

Ink sauce:

1 to 1¼ pounds	squid *with ink*
3 tablespoons	finely chopped shallots
⅓ cup	diced tomatoes
1⅓ cups	fish stock (see page 27)
	Salt and freshly ground pepper

Garnish:

8	crayfish, poached for 2 minutes, tails removed
About ½ pound	tiny broccoli florets, washed and blanched for 15 seconds

○ To make the sausages, purée the salmon trout in a food processor. Chill in a bowl over ice and gradually beat in the tofu, a little at a time. Season well with salt and pepper and chill until required.

○ Open the oysters and remove oysters from shells carefully, saving their liquid.

○ Mix oysters with dill and chilled salmon trout mousse and, if necessary, season with lemon juice, salt, and pepper.

○ Put the mixture of mousse and whole oysters into a pastry bag and fill the sausage casings. Tie with string to make four sausages. Chill until required.

○ To make the saffron sauce, put the fish stock and shallots in a pan and reduce stock by half by rapid boiling.

○ Add the saffron and fromage blanc and mix in well.

○ Bring to a boil again and pass through a fine sieve. Season to taste.

○ To make the ink sauce, remove the ink sacs from the bodies of the fish. Separate the heads from the bodies and wash well (save the meat for another dish).

○ Sweat the finely chopped shallots in a nonstick pan. Add the ink pouches, squid heads, and tomatoes and sweat for a further 3 to 4 minutes.

○ Add fish stock and oyster liquor, cover, and simmer for 5 minutes. Pass through a fine sieve, bring to the boil again, and season with salt and pepper.

○ Poach the oyster sausages in water for 3 minutes, and sauté broccoli and crayfish tails quickly in a nonstick pan.

○ To serve, pour the hot yellow saffron sauce gently onto half of each of four individual plates. Cover the other half of the plate with the hot black ink sauce. Place the oyster sausages in the middle of the two sauces, where they meet. Garnish with the warm, seasoned crayfish and broccoli florets.

RAVIOLI WITH SPINACH AND PARSLEY SAUCE
Ravioli aux épinards et sauce persil

SERVES 4

3 tablespoons	finely chopped shallots
½ pound	spinach leaves, well washed, thick stems removed, and blanched
1	clove garlic, peeled and crushed
1	egg, beaten
¼ cup	cottage cheese
	A pinch of grated nutmeg
	Salt and freshly ground pepper
1 recipe	of ravioli dough (see page 35)
	Beaten egg to seal

Parsley sauce:

4 to 5 bunches	of flat-leafed parsley (about ½ pound), stems removed
¼ cup	finely chopped shallots
1⅓ cups	white veal stock (see page 20)
¼ cup	fromage blanc (see page 29)
	Juice of ½ lemon
	Salt and freshly ground pepper

○ Sauté the shallots in a nonstick pan without browning.

○ Chop the spinach finely and add to the shallots with the garlic. Cook for 1 to 2 minutes.

○ Remove from the heat and beat in the egg, cheese, and seasonings.

○ Roll out half the ravioli dough until thin, then arrange teaspoonfuls of the mixture at regular intervals about 1 inch apart.

○ Brush between each spoonful of filling with beaten egg.

○ Roll out the remaining dough to a similar size and carefully place on top of the first sheet.

○ Press firmly between the mounds of filling to make each square of ravioli. Cut in between each one with a sharp knife.

○ To make the sauce, place parsley in a saucepan with the shallots and half the stock. Bring to the boil, reduce heat, cover, and simmer for 5 minutes.

○ Add the fromage blanc and lemon juice and process in a blender or food processor, adding the remaining stock gradually to give the required consistency—nice and runny. Season to taste with salt and pepper.

○ Cook ravioli in boiling salted water for 3 to 4 minutes. Drain, rinse in boiling water, and serve at once with hot parsley sauce.

TORTELLINI WITH FRESH BEET FILLING
Tortellini farci à la betterave

Using a double quantity of ravioli dough, make these tortellini in whatever color you like—black, red, green, brown, or white—and freeze any remainder. (See methods for coloring homemade noodles.) *Mix* the colors, too, if preferred.

To vary the tortellini shape, you could cut out 2¼-inch squares instead of circles. Place 1 teaspoon of filling in the middle of each square and brush the edges with egg white. Press diagonally opposite corners together over the filling, then press down the other facing corners in the same way. Press all edges together so that the filling is completely enclosed. Cook as below.

SERVES 10

Double recipe of ravioli dough (see page 35)

Filling:

¼ pound	beets, cooked and peeled
2	carrots, cooked
2	stalks of celery, cooked
1	slice of whole wheat bread, without crust, about 1¼ ounces, soaked in ¼ cup hot water and squeezed out
1	egg, separated
⅓ cup	finely cut chives
	Salt and freshly ground pepper
¼ cup	fromage blanc (see page 29)
2 to 3	sage leaves, finely cut
1 teaspoon	poppy seeds
1	clove of garlic, peeled and finely chopped
4 ounces	Parmesan cheese, freshly grated

○ To make the filling, cut the beets, carrots, and celery into cubes and purée with the bread in a food processor or blender.

○ Add the egg yolk and chives, mix, and season to taste with salt and pepper.

○ Roll out the dough thinly on a floured surface and cut out 2-inch circles.

○ Place 1 teaspoon of the filling in the middle of each circle of dough, brush the edges with the egg white, and fold the circles in half. Press the edges together well.

○ Carefully make the semicircles into circle shapes around the fingers so that both ends touch. With the other hand, bend the firmly pressed edges of the dough upward.

○ Cook the tortellini in plenty of boiling salted water, a portion at a time, until *al dente* (until they float on top of the water), then drain.

○ Heat the fromage blanc in a pan and add the sage leaves, poppy seeds, and garlic.

○ Add the tortellini, mix well, and season to taste. Heat gently through.

○ To serve, put onto four individual plates and sprinkle with the grated Parmesan.

HOMEMADE EGG NOODLES
Nouilles aux oeufs frais

Noodles are fairly simple to make at home and taste very superior to the
bought varieties. They can be flavored and colored in many ways, as you
can see from the suggestions below. For a stunning presentation, serve
a selection of colored noodles (see photograph opposite).
Noodles must always be cooked *al dente*. After draining, rinse with
hot water, toss in a little warmed fromage blanc, season, and serve
immediately.
Freshly cut herbs such as basil or chives may be added.

SERVES 4

1½ cups	all-purpose flour (or fine whole wheat flour), sifted
Scant ¼ cup	semolina
1	egg
	A pinch of salt
4 tablespoons	hot water

○ Mix the flour and semolina together and make a well in the center.

○ Place the other ingredients in the well.

○ Gradually work the flour and semolina in toward the middle and knead into a
very firm, smooth dough.

○ Wrap in a damp cloth and allow to rest in a cool place for at least 2 to 3 hours.

○ Divide the dough into five pieces and roll out each piece as thinly as possible. Lay
the pieces on top of each other and cut into strips approximately ¼ inch wide.

○ An alternative method of cutting is to roll the five pieces of dough into thin
circles. Fold each circle in loosely from both sides, parallel to the middle. Do this
again until both folded edges meet in the middle. Then cut the dough into strips.

○ These noodles may be cooked while fresh or left to dry out. Boil for 2 to 3
minutes if fresh, for about double that time if dried.

○ If whole wheat flour is used instead of plain, the pasta will be brown, not white.

HOMEMADE EGG NOODLES WITH INK
Nouilles à l'encre

1½ cups	all-purpose flour, sifted
Scant ¼ cup	semolina
1	egg
	A pinch of salt
3 tablespoons	reduced squid ink, plus a little warm water if necessary

Buy very fresh squid with unbroken ink sacs, so that as much ink as possible can be collected. About 2 pounds of squid should provide enough ink to reduce, by simmering, to the required quantity of 3 tablespoons. If necessary, make up the amount with a little warm water. (Use the squid meat in Squid Salad, see page 41.)

Add ink, or ink and water, to the flour mixture instead of the hot water in the recipe for Homemade Egg Noodles, along with the egg.

HOMEMADE EGG NOODLES WITH SAFFRON
Nouilles au safran

1½ cups	all-purpose flour, sifted
Scant ¼ cup	semolina
1	egg
	A pinch of salt
	A large pinch of saffron strands or powder

Blanch the saffron in 3 to 4 tablespoons hot water. When a deep yellow, add the strained liquid to the flour mixture instead of the hot water in the recipe for Homemade Egg Noodles, along with the egg.

HOMEMADE EGG NOODLES
WITH SPINACH
Nouilles aux épinards

1½ cups	all-purpose flour, sifted
Scant ¼ cup	semolina
1	egg
	A pinch of salt
3 to 4 tablespoons	spinach purée, plus a little warm water if necessary

Wash about ¾ pound spinach leaves thoroughly and cut away thick stems. Blanch quickly, then refresh in cold water. Chop very finely or purée in a blender or food processor. Add 3 to 4 tablespoons of this purée, with a little warm water if necessary, to the flour mixture instead of the hot water in the recipe for Homemade Egg Noodles, along with the egg.

HOMEMADE EGG NOODLES
WITH TOMATO
Nouilles aux tomates

1½ cups	all-purpose flour, sifted
Scant ¼ cup	semolina
1	egg
	A pinch of salt
3 to 4 tablespoons	tomato coulis (see page 141)

Add the tomato coulis, with a little warm water if necessary, to the flour mixture instead of the hot water in the recipe for Homemade Egg Noodles, along with the egg.

SOUPS

Soups are becoming fashionable again after many years of apparent culinary disfavor. It is a welcome reappearance because soups can be good for health, can look and taste spectacular, and are very versatile. A bowl of a vegetable soup or chowder could be a light lunch—with some whole wheat bread as the ideal healthy accompaniment—or the first course of a simpler two- or three-course meal; a perfectly clear consommé garnished with colorful vegetable dice and medallions of seafood could be served after the appetizer and before the main course. A cold soup is the perfect start to a meal on a hot day.

The soups in this brief chapter—ranging from the most sophisticated lobster consommé to a nourishing, protein-rich lentil soup—encompass par excellence all the principles of Cuisine Naturelle: using the best ingredients and made without butter, oil, cream, or alcohol.

The basis of any good soup, though, is the best stock, and, although many of the soup recipes hold instructions for their own individual stock or consommé, there are inevitable cross-references to the chapter on stocks.

To cut down on salt, a relevant herb mixture from the selection on page 36 could be used instead of some salt in all the soup recipes.

DIALOGUE OF FRUIT PUREES
Dialogue de purées de fruits

This marbling of purées looks spectacular. It can be served in summer
as a first-course soup, as a sherbet between courses, or as a dessert.
The idea was created by the famous German chef Hans Peter Wodarz,
who is a great friend.

SERVES 4

½ pound	kiwi fruit, peeled
About 1 pound	mangoes, peeled and pitted
1 pint	strawberries, cleaned
1⅔ cups	currants, cleaned and stemmed
2	medium apples, peeled and cored
1 pint	raspberries
	Juice of ½ lemon
½ cup	mineral water
	A little superfine sugar
	A little apple juice
	Wild strawberries (or raspberries) and tiny sprigs of mint for garnish

○ Carefully crush the kiwi fruit with a fork (the black pips should not be broken).
Remove pips and strain the purée through a fine sieve. Thin down a little with
mineral water if necessary. Chill.

○ Purée the mango flesh in a food processor or blender. Strain as above and thin
down with mineral water if necessary. Chill.

○ Purée the strawberries in a food processor or blender, strain as above, and season
well with a little lemon juice and sugar. Chill.

○ Bring the currants to the boil in water with a little lemon juice and sugar. Allow
to cool, then purée and strain through a fine sieve. Thin with a little mineral water
if necessary. Chill.

○ Cook the apples until very soft in a minimum of water with a little lemon juice
and sugar. Allow to cool, then strain through a fine sieve. If necessary thin the
purée down with a little apple juice so that it has the same consistency as the kiwi
purée. Chill.

○ Purée the raspberries in a food processor or blender and strain through a fine
sieve. Strengthen the raspberry flavor with lemon juice and sugar. If necessary,
thin down with mineral water. Chill.

○ To serve, put a scoop of each very cold purée into a soup plate, arranging them around the plate, with the darkest one in the middle. Knock the plate firmly (not *too* firmly, or you may break it) on a solid surface, so that the purées blend together at the edges. Garnish with a wild strawberry and mint.

COLD VEGETABLE SOUP
WITH BASIL
Potage froid des meilleurs légumes du potager

SERVES 4

2 pounds	ripe red tomatoes, seeded and diced
1	large cucumber, seeded and diced
⅓ cup	finely diced onion
½	red pepper, diced
1	clove of garlic, peeled and crushed
½ cup	fresh brown bread crumbs
8 teaspoons	red wine vinegar
1 cup	vegetable stock (see page 26)
	A few sprigs of oregano
16	basil leaves
	Salt and freshly ground pepper

○ Mix together the tomatoes, cucumber, onion, red pepper, garlic, and bread crumbs.

○ Add the vinegar, stock, oregano, and twelve of the basil leaves.

○ Marinate for 12 hours.

○ Purée in a blender and season to taste.

○ Serve cold, garnished with the remaining basil leaves.

FISHERMAN'S CLAM CHOWDER

This chowder can also be served cold.

SERVES 4

24	cherrystone clams
3½ cups	fish stock (see page 27)
3 tablespoons	each of finely diced onion, leek, and carrot
6 tablespoons	finely diced celeriac
1	clove of garlic, peeled and crushed
1	small bay leaf
3 tablespoons	finely diced green pepper
1	medium potato, cut in small dice
2	tomatoes, halved, seeded, and diced
1 teaspoon	chopped fresh thyme
1 teaspoon	chopped parsley
	Salt and freshly ground pepper

○ Scrub the clams and place in a large pan with the stock. Cover and simmer until the clams open. Remove from the stock and let cool. Strain the stock through cheesecloth or a fine sieve and reserve.

○ Remove the "beard" from the clams and chop the flesh.

○ Sauté the onion, leek, carrot, celeriac, and garlic in a nonstick pan without browning.

○ Add the bay leaf, green pepper, potato, and reserved stock and simmer for about 5 minutes.

○ Add the clams and the tomatoes and simmer for a further 5 minutes. Remove bay leaf.

○ Add herbs and season to taste with salt and pepper.

FISH SOUP WITH CRAB AND MELON
Bouillon de poissons au crabe et melon

Only the white meat of the crab is used for this soup. Use the dark meat in another dish such as crab salad or canapé toppings. The crab-flavored court bouillon can be kept, too, for another dish (best frozen). I used honeydew melon for the soup, but any melon in season is suitable.

SERVES 4

1	crab, about 1¼ pounds
4 quarts	court bouillon (see page 28)
5 cups	clear fish stock (see page 27)
2 teaspoons	soy sauce
	Freshly ground pepper
½ pound	ripe melon flesh
4	thin slices of peeled lemon
	Fresh coriander or chervil leaves

○ Brush and wash the crab, put into boiling court bouillon, and cook for 10 minutes.

○ Allow to cool in the court bouillon, then break open the crab and carefully remove the meat.

○ Slowly reduce the fish stock by half, then season with the soy sauce and freshly ground pepper. Strain through a cheesecloth.

○ Cut the melon flesh into small pieces of equal size, or use a melon baller.

○ Warm the white crab meat and pieces of melon in a little stock, then arrange in soup dishes.

○ Pour in the well-seasoned fish stock. Add the lemon slices and serve immediately, garnished with coriander or chervil leaves.

CRAYFISH AND CHICKEN SOUP WITH CHERVIL

Petite marmite d'écrevisses et de volaille

SERVES 4

2	raw chicken carcasses, with giblets
⅓ cup	*each* of diced onion, carrot, leek, and celery
About ½ cup	*each* of julienned onion, carrot, leek, and celery
1	sprig of thyme
1	sprig of rosemary
7 cups	water
16	live crayfish
1	chicken breast, skinned and boned
	Salt and freshly ground pepper
	Small bunch of chervil to garnish

○ Roughly chop the chicken carcasses and place in a large pan.

○ Add the diced vegetables with the thyme, rosemary, and water. Bring to the boil, reduce heat, then simmer for 1 hour.

○ Meanwhile, blanch the crayfish for 1 minute in a minimum of boiling salted water. Leave in the cooking liquid, but place pan in a bowl of ice.

○ When cool, remove the tails from the crayfish. Reserve and roughly chop all the shells.

○ Strain the chicken stock through a cheesecloth and remove any fat. Return to a clean saucepan.

○ Poach the crayfish tails in the stock for 2 minutes, then remove from the pan.

○ Add the crushed shells to the stock and simmer for 10 minutes.

○ Strain the stock into a clean pan and poach the chicken breast for 5 minutes until just pink. Remove from the pan.

○ Add the julienne of vegetables to the pan and cook for 1 minute.

○ Cut the chicken breast into julienne strips, then add to the pan along with the crayfish tails.

○ Warm through, without boiling. Check seasoning, then serve at once, garnished with sprigs of chervil.

SCALLOP SOUP
FLAVORED WITH GINGER
Potage aux coquilles St. Jacques parfumé au gingembre

SERVES 4

12	sea scallops
1 ounce	fresh ginger
2	large scallions
2½ cups	fish stock (see page 27)
½ tablespoon	soy sauce
½ teaspoon	arrowroot (or cornstarch)
	A dash of lemon juice
	Salt and freshly ground pepper

○ Cut the scallops into strips ⅛ inch thick.

○ Peel the ginger and reserve the trimmings. Cut the ginger into fine julienne strips. Place in cold water, bring to the boil, drain, and reserve.

○ Finely slice the scallions.

○ Place the ginger trimmings in the fish stock. Bring to the boil and leave to infuse for 15 minutes. Strain through fine cheesecloth into a clean pan.

○ Add the soy sauce, julienne of ginger, and shredded scallions to the strained stock and bring to simmering point.

○ Mix the arrowroot (or cornstarch) with a little water and stir into the stock. Season to taste with lemon juice, salt, and pepper.

○ Season the scallop strips, add them to the soup, and poach for 10 seconds. Serve at once.

LOBSTER CONSOMME WITH CORIANDER LEAVES
Consommé de homard aux feuilles de coriandre

This is a very unusual consommé but well worth the effort—it is a wonderful combination in both flavor and color. Female lobsters are used because they are much more flavorful and because the coral and eggs are used in the garnish.

SERVES 10

2	live female lobsters, about ¾ pound each
3 quarts	court bouillon (see page 28)

Basic stock:

3¼ pounds	lobster shells, chopped, with claws and body meat
1	large leek
2	carrots
2	stalks of celery ⎫ cut in small cubes
1	tomato
½	onion
1	clove
5 quarts	fish stock (see page 27)
	Salt and freshly ground pepper

To clarify:

About 1 pound	white fish fillets, skinned, boned, and minced
1	tomato
1	leek
1	stalk of celery ⎫ cut in small cubes
1	carrot
6	coriander stems
3	tarragon stems
2	egg whites, whisked until frothy
10 to 12	ice cubes

Garnish:

20	small lobster medallions (cut from tails of above)
3	carrots ⎫ thinly sliced and cut into lobster shapes, then
2	stalks of celery ⎭ blanched in lightly salted water for 15 seconds
30 to 40	enoki mushrooms
20 to 30	fresh coriander leaves
2 to 2½ tablespoons	(1½ ounces) lobster roe, blanched in a minimum of water with 1 tablespoon vinegar added

○ Splash the live lobsters with cold water, then plunge into the boiling court bouillon for 2 minutes. Remove from heat and leave to cool in court bouillon, the pan sitting in a large bowl of ice to speed up the process.

○ Shell the lobsters and retain meat for garnish. Put shells on baking sheet in a moderate oven (350° F) for about 20 minutes until dry. This helps to bring out the flavor.

○ Place lobster shells and all remaining ingredients for the basic stock in a large saucepan or casserole.

○ Bring to the boil, skimming from time to time. Allow to simmer for 45 minutes, still skimming occasionally.

○ Pass carefully through a sieve and allow to cool.

○ To clarify the stock, mix the ingredients listed together with the ice cubes.

○ Place in a large saucepan and add the stock. Bring to the boil, whisking constantly, and then allow to simmer for 45 minutes.

○ Pass through a fine cheesecloth-lined sieve and season to taste with salt and pepper.

○ Pour the consommé into soup plates or cups and garnish with the lobster medallions, carrot and celery shapes, enoki mushrooms, coriander leaves, and lobster roe. Serve immediately.

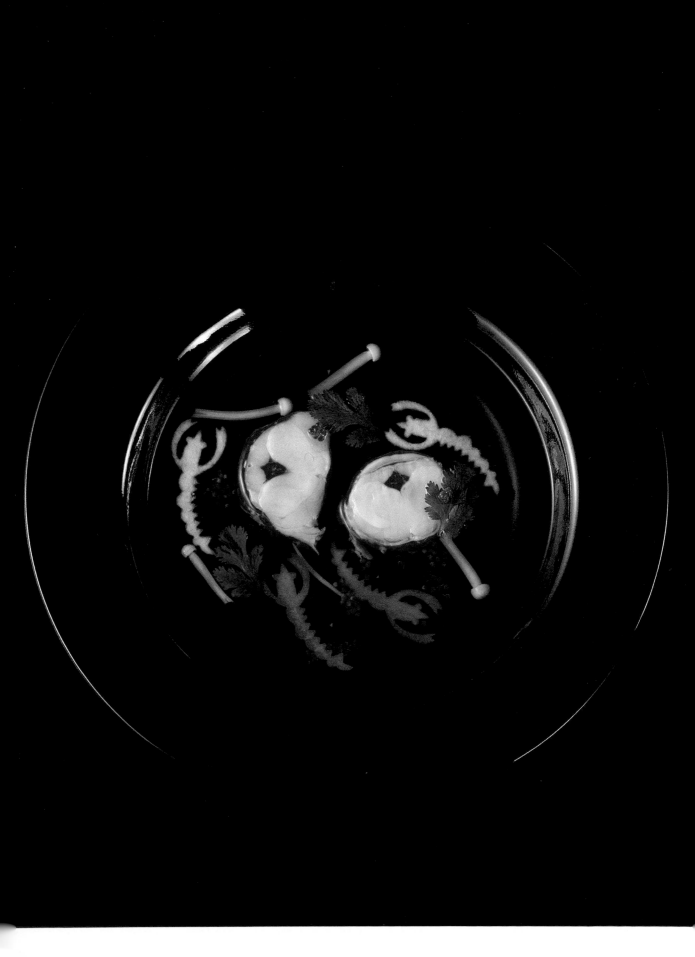

POTATO AND WATERCRESS SOUP
WITH MUSSELS
Potage au cresson et moules

SERVES 4

¼ cup	finely chopped shallots
1	clove of garlic, peeled and finely chopped
1	medium leek, washed and finely cut
¾ pound	potatoes, peeled and diced
2	bunches of watercress, tough stems removed
2¼ cups	strong fish stock (see page 27)
2¼ cups	strong white poultry stock (see page 19)
	Salt and freshly ground pepper

For the mussels:

About 1¼ pounds	mussels
⅓ cup	*each* of finely chopped leeks, carrots, and celery
1	sprig of thyme
1	clove of garlic, unpeeled and crushed
⅔ cup	fish stock (see page 27)

○ Sweat the shallots and garlic gently in a nonstick pan.

○ Add the leek, potatoes, and watercress leaves, reserving twelve leaves for garnish.

○ Sweat until soft without allowing the ingredients to brown, then add the stocks and bring to the boil.

○ Purée the soup in a blender or food processor, pour into a saucepan, and season.

○ Wash the mussels thoroughly and remove the beards.

○ Sweat the cut vegetables, thyme, and garlic in a large nonstick pan for about 2 minutes, then add the mussels.

○ Add the fish stock and cook until the mussels open.

○ Remove and discard the shells and place the mussels in the puréed soup. Warm through quickly and garnish with watercress leaves just before serving.

CHICKEN CONSOMME WITH WHITE ASPARAGUS AND BLACK TRUFFLES

Consommé de poulet aux asperges blanches et truffes noires

SERVES 10

2	raw chicken carcasses, about 2 pounds
2	onions with skins
5 quarts	water
2	cloves
¼	bay leaf
1	medium leek, cleaned and roughly cut
½	stalk of celery, roughly cut
	Juice of 1 lemon

To clarify:

About 1 pound	raw chicken leg meat, minced
3	egg whites, whisked until frothy
1	tomato, chopped
2	sprigs of fresh tarragon

Garnish:

30	small tips of white asparagus, well blanched
30	thin slices of black truffle
30	sprigs of chervil

○ Blanch the chicken carcasses in boiling water for 1 minute.

○ Remove and rinse the carcasses under cold running water.

○ Halve the onions and place the cut sides on a hot nonstick pan, or broil them until dark brown.

○ Add all the ingredients for the stock to the pan. Bring to the boil, reduce heat, and simmer for 1½ hours.

○ Strain through cheesecloth. Return to a clean pan.

○ To clarify the stock, stir together the ingredients listed and whisk into the warm stock. Bring slowly to the boil, whisking all the time. When it comes to the boil, stop whisking, reduce heat, and simmer for 45 minutes.

○ Line a sieve or colander with a fine cloth and spoon the froth into it. Pour the stock through this froth. It will be completely clear. Remove fat by dragging strips of paper towels over the surface of the consommé.

○ Heat to serving temperature, spoon into soup plates, and garnish with asparagus tips, truffle slices, and tiny sprigs of chervil.

QUAIL CONSOMME WITH CHERVIL
Consommé de cailles au cerfeuil

A consommé similar to this can be made from any other game bird or chicken. The breasts for the garnish have to be pink so that they are tender.

SERVES 10

1¼ pounds	quail and game bird carcasses, giblets, and skin, chopped
¾ pounds	veal knuckle, chopped
5 quarts	water
	Salt
1	clove
1	medium onion, unpeeled, cut in half, and well browned on a griddle or in a hot pan
½	bay leaf
2	carrots
1	large leek } cut in small cubes
2	stalks of celery

To clarify:

About ½ pound	raw quail leg meat, coarsely minced
About ½ pound	poultry meat, coarsely minced
3	egg whites *or* 10 quail egg whites, whisked until frothy
1	medium tomato, coarsely chopped
¼ pound	celeriac, cut into small pieces
1	bunch parsley stalks, without the leaves
	A few chervil stems
	Salt and freshly ground pepper

Garnish:

10	quail breasts, bones removed but skin retained
3	carrots } sliced thinly, then cut into chicken shapes and blanched
2	stalks of celery } in slightly salted water for 15 seconds
10	quail egg yolks (keep each one separate)
80	chervil leaves

○ Carefully sauté the quail and game bird bones, giblets and skin, and veal knuckle in a nonstick pan for about 15 minutes.

○ Transfer to a large casserole or pan and add the water and a pinch of salt. Bring to the boil. Skim, then allow to simmer for 20 minutes.

○ Push the clove into the browned onion and add to the stock, with the bay leaf.

○ Add the carrots, leek, and celery.

○ Simmer for a further 45 minutes, skimming from time to time.

○ Strain carefully through a fine cloth and allow stock to cool.

○ To clarify the stock, mix the quail and poultry meat with the egg whites, tomatoes, celeriac, parsley, and chervil stems.

○ Add all this to the stock and bring to the boil, whisking constantly. Allow to simmer for 30 minutes.

○ Pass through a fine cheesecloth-lined sieve and remove any fat with paper towels. Season with salt and pepper.

○ Sauté the quail breasts for the garnish in a nonstick pan for about 1 minute, turning once, until still pink. Remove the skin and slice the breasts carefully.

○ Pour the consommé into soup plates and garnish with the quail breast slices, vegetable garnish, raw egg yolks, and chervil (8 leaves per plate). Serve immediately.

BEEF AND LENTIL SOUP
Soupe à lentilles

Lentils are an ancient food, almost as rich in protein as soybeans. They contain no fat but have a high carbohydrate content—so a bowl of this soup, with only a piece of good whole wheat bread as accompaniment, makes a nourishing meal.

SERVES 4

3 ounces	lean shoulder of beef, cut into small dice
	Salt and freshly ground pepper
½	medium onion, finely chopped
½	medium leek, cut into strips
1	carrot, diced
5 ounces	lentils, soaked overnight
7 cups	meat broth (see page 18)
½	bay leaf
1 teaspoon	chopped fresh thyme

○ Season the beef with salt and pepper and sauté it carefully in a nonstick pan until well browned on all sides.

○ Add the onion, leek, and carrot and sauté, stirring occasionally, until the onion is transparent.

○ Add the soaked, drained lentils, broth, bay leaf, and thyme. Cover and simmer gently for about 1 hour until meat and lentils are tender.

○ Season to taste with salt and pepper, and remove bay leaf before serving.

LEEK AND ONION SOUP
Potage de poireaux et oignons

SERVES 4

1⅓ cups   finely chopped onions
1⅓ cups   finely cut leeks
½ cup   brown veal stock (see page 22)
2½ cups   meat broth (see page 18)
            Salt and freshly ground pepper
            A little coarsely chopped parsley for garnish

○ Sweat the onions and leeks carefully in a nonstick pan until golden, stirring constantly. Transfer to a saucepan.

○ Add the brown veal stock and simmer for 5 minutes to reduce a little.

○ Add the meat broth and allow to simmer for 8 to 10 minutes longer.

○ Season with salt and pepper and garnish with the parsley before serving.

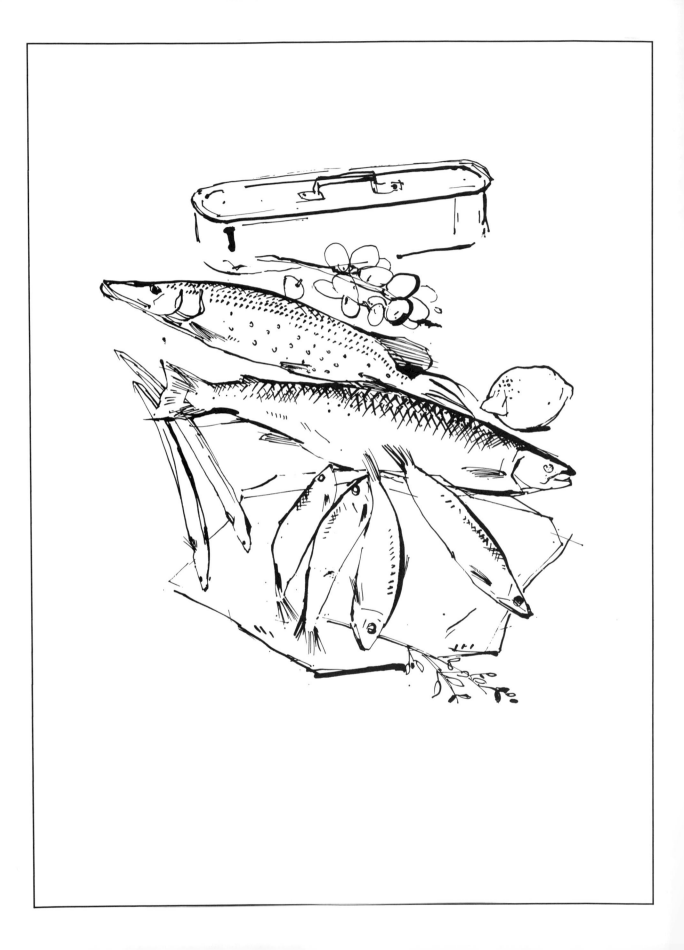

FISH

Fish has undoubtedly become the favorite ingredient of the modern creative kitchen. A fresh, flavorful fish contains proteins and many of the vitamins and minerals not freely available elsewhere (vitamin D, in oily fish, and iodine, for example). Fish is also easily digested and desirable for good health. White fish, particularly, has a low fat content and contains relatively few calories.

Fish is valued, too, for its variety, versatility, and flavor. With an increasing interest in health, and thus in fish as a major source of protein, markets should make available an enormous variety of fish. With a few exceptions, fish come mostly from the wild. Depending on the water in which they live—and also, sadly, upon the degree of pollution in that water—their flesh develops a special character in both texture and taste. Thus there is an even wider choice. Always choose the freshest fish—look for clear eyes, red gills, firm flesh and scales. The smell from the open gills should be fresh, not "fishy." Try to avoid buying fish shortly before and after the spawning season because they are then generally less tasty.

Fish is also incredibly versatile—in methods of cookery, flavor, and usage—and lends itself admirably to the basics of Cuisine Naturelle—preferring indeed the processes, particularly steaming, that are central to Cuisine Naturelle. Although in general, fewer sauces are used, many of the simplest vegetable sauces, natural and true in flavor, are more complementary than richer cream- or butter-based sauces.

Take care never to overcook fish or to cook it at too high a temperature. At temperatures above 104° F, animal proteins start to coagulate, to congeal (reminiscent of the protein in eggs). At approximately 122° F, 40 to 50 percent of the protein has congealed, and at 176° F the flavor-holding juices run out, and the fish becomes dry and tasteless. The recipes in this section specify exact timings; these may appear short but should be followed meticulously for total success.

Never leave fish soaking in water because this leaches out flavor as well as the protein, vitamins, and minerals. Always use the best stocks for giving flavor to fish sauces and for poaching. The simplest of accompaniments and garnishes are all that are needed.

To cut salt consumption in the following fish recipes, try a pinch or two of the fish herb mixture on page 36; this should reduce the need for salt by about half.

STEAMED SEA BASS, CHINESE STYLE
Loup de mer à la chinoise

SERVES 4

1	sea bass, about 2¼ pounds, cleaned
2 tablespoons	lemon juice
3 tablespoons	light soy sauce
	Freshly ground pepper
4	scallions, trimmed and cut into 2- to 3-inch lengths
10	snowpeas
1	large carrot, peeled
3	cloves of garlic, peeled
1	slice of fresh ginger, about ¼ inch thick, peeled
1 cup	fish stock (see page 27)
1 teaspoon	cornstarch
1 to 2 tablespoons	water
1	large egg, beaten

○ With a sharp knife cut four or five diagonal slashes on each side of the fish.

○ Stir together 1 tablespoon each of lemon juice and soy sauce.

○ Sprinkle a little of this into each of the slashes and rub into the flesh inside and out. Season the fish with the pepper.

○ Cut the scallion lengths into julienne and press half into the slashes in the fish. Reserve the others.

○ To prepare the sauce, cut the snowpeas and carrot into julienne strips; crush the garlic and ginger; and mix together the stock and the remaining lemon juice and soy sauce.

○ Steam the fish for about 10 to 12 minutes until the flesh along the backbone is opaque.

○ Meanwhile, make the sauce. Stir together the cornstarch and water. Sauté the garlic and ginger in a nonstick pan for 10 seconds, then add the reserved vegetables and cook, stirring until the color brightens.

○ Pour in the reserved stock and water and cornstarch and cook until thickened, stirring continuously.

○ Add the egg, stirring all the time, and remove from the heat immediately.

○ Remove the fish from the steamer, transfer to a plate, and spoon the sauce over. Serve at once.

STEAMED SARDINES
WITH FRESH CORIANDER LEAVES
Délice de sardines à la vapeur

Sardines are now commonly available other than in cans and, steamed
in this fashion, as opposed to broiling or baking, are delicious.

SERVES 4

8	sardines, cleaned and scales removed
	Freshly ground pepper
4 teaspoons	lemon juice
1 teaspoon	sugar
4 teaspoons	soy sauce
2	thin slices fresh ginger, peeled and cut into fine julienne strips
	Fresh coriander leaves to garnish

○ Season the sardines with pepper and steam for 4 to 5 minutes.

○ Place the lemon juice, sugar, soy sauce, and ginger julienne in a saucepan and bring to a simmer.

○ Arrange the sardines on individual plates, spoon a little sauce over each fish, and garnish with coriander leaves.

SALMON TROUT STEAKS
BAKED IN THEIR OWN JUICES
Steaks de truites saumonées dans leurs jus

Always open and serve the "packages" in front of the guests because
only then are the full taste and aroma appreciated.

SERVES 4

1½ pounds	fillet of salmon trout, skinned	
	Salt and freshly ground pepper	
½	medium onion	
1	large carrot	cut into thin
½	large leek	julienne strips
¼ pound	mushrooms	
12	tarragon leaves	
8 teaspoons	fish stock (see page 27)	

○ Carefully remove any bones from the salmon trout and cut into four steaks. Season with salt and pepper.

○ Sweat the onion in a nonstick pan without browning until it is transparent.

○ Add the carrot and leek and continue to sweat for a further 2 minutes.

○ Finally, add the mushrooms and sweat for another minute.

○ Add four tarragon leaves and season with salt and pepper.

○ Have ready four pieces of greaseproof paper about three times as large as each salmon trout steak and divide the vegetables among them.

○ Arrange the seasoned steaks on top of the vegetables and garnish with remaining tarragon leaves.

○ Dribble a little fish stock over each steak, then carefully fold the foil edges together to make an airtight pouch.

○ Place on a baking sheet, and bake in a moderate oven (325° F) for 8 to 10 minutes.

FILLET OF SALMON
WITH WATERCRESS
Suprême de saumon au cresson

SERVES 4

About 1¼ pounds | fillet of salmon, cut into 4 pieces
2 tablespoons | shallots, chopped
⅞ cup | fish stock (see page 27)

Mousseline of pike:

1 | bunch of watercress, stems removed
5 ounces | fillet of pike (or whiting, angler, or turbot), chilled
1 | egg white, chilled
| Pinch of salt
⅝ cup | fromage blanc, chilled (see page 29)
| Salt and freshly ground pepper

○ For the mousseline, blanch the watercress leaves in boiling salted water. Refresh in ice water and drain well.

○ Purée the pike fillet in a food processor with the watercress, then add the egg white and a pinch of salt, and purée until thick and smooth.

○ Place the fish mixture in a bowl over a bowl of ice. Beat in the fromage blanc, a little at a time. Season well. Leave the mixture in the ice until required.

○ Season the salmon fillets with salt and pepper, then spread a quarter of the mousseline over each one.

○ Place the shallots and fish stock in a gratin dish and arrange the salmon fillets in the stock, mousseline side up.

○ Cover and poach gently for 5 to 7 minutes. Remove from the stock and keep warm.

○ Reduce the stock by half by boiling rapidly. Strain and spoon around the fish on individual serving plates.

SALMON SUPREME
WITH BLACK NOODLES
Suprême de saumon aux nouilles noires

The very unusual black noodles in this recipe—made with squid ink—
accompany the salmon perfectly.

SERVES 4

4	fillets of salmon, about 5 ounces each, boned and skinned
	Salt and freshly ground pepper
4	sprigs of basil
4	sheets filo dough (see page 34)
2½ tablespoons	finely chopped shallots
2 teaspoons	finely chopped garlic
About ½ pound	ripe tomatoes, peeled, seeded, and diced
1 tablespoon	cut chives
1	recipe black noodles (see page 79)

○ Season the salmon fillets with salt and pepper and place a sprig of basil on top of each.

○ Blanch each sheet of filo dough by dipping briefly in boiling water, then in cold water. Remove immediately.

○ Wrap each salmon fillet in a blanched filo sheet.

○ Steam fillets for 3 to 4 minutes.

○ Sauté the shallots and garlic in a nonstick pan, stirring constantly, until transparent.

○ Add the tomatoes and sauté for about 1 minute.

○ Add the cut chives and season with salt and pepper.

○ Cook the black noodles in boiling salted water for about 3 minutes until *al dente*.

○ Drain the noodles, reserving 2 tablespoons cooking water, and rinse quickly in cold water. Toss the noodles with the reserved water in a saucepan over gentle heat, then season with salt and pepper.

○ Put the noodles on four individual plates and arrange the salmon on top. Make a small cut in the top of the pastry and gently ease out one of the basil leaves from the sprig. Garnish with the well-seasoned tomatoes.

FILLET OF HALIBUT
WITH TWO SAUCES
Fillet de flétan aux deux sauces

Vegetable sauces marry happily with fish because they are natural in flavor, do not overpower the flavor of the fish itself, and look good.

SERVES 4

2	large yellow peppers
2	large red peppers
3 tablespoons	finely chopped shallots
2	small cloves of garlic, peeled and crushed
	A few sprigs of thyme
2½ cups	fish stock (see page 27), plus about 1 cup for steaming
	Salt and freshly ground pepper
4	fillets of halibut, about 5 ounces each, skinned and boned

○ Wash and trim the peppers and cut into large pieces.

○ Sweat the shallots and garlic in a nonstick frying pan over gentle heat without browning.

○ Divide the shallot mixture between two saucepans.

○ Add the yellow peppers to one pan and the red peppers to the other.

○ Divide the thyme and the 2½ cups fish stock between the two pans. Cover and simmer for 15 minutes until tender.

○ Process each mixture in a blender until smooth, strain if desired, then season to taste with salt and pepper.

○ Season the halibut with salt and pepper and steam over the remaining 1 cup fish stock for 4 to 5 minutes.

○ Arrange the two well-seasoned hot sauces carefully on the plates (see the photograph opposite). Top with the fish and serve at once.

GRILLED MONKFISH TAILS
WITH FRESH HERBS
Queues de lotte grillées aux herbes

Monkfish used to be undervalued and cheap but has now gained the recognition it deserves because of its good, firm texture. It can be prepared in a variety of ways.

SERVES 4

4   small monkfish tails, about 8 ounces each, with bone
      Juice of ½ lemon
⅓ cup   freshly chopped and cut mixed herbs (such as dill, basil, thyme, marjoram)
1   small clove of garlic, peeled and crushed
      Salt and freshly ground pepper
      Parsley sprigs and lemon wedges to garnish

○ Carefully remove any skin from the fish tails and trim well.

○ Sprinkle the fish with lemon juice, herbs, and garlic and leave to absorb the flavors for about an hour.

○ Remove the fish from the marinade, season with salt and pepper, and grill on both sides for about 8 to 10 minutes, turning once.

○ Arrange on a serving dish and garnish with parsley and lemon.

○ Serve with tomato concassé (page 33) if desired.

MONKFISH RAGOUT WITH TOMATOES
Ragoût de lotte sans nom

SERVES 4

About 1¼ pounds	fillet of monkfish
	Juice of 1 lemon
1	small clove of garlic, peeled and crushed
1	sprig *each* of dill and rosemary, cut and chopped
6	basil leaves, finely cut
3 tablespoons	chopped parsley
	Salt and freshly ground pepper
2	onions, peeled and finely sliced
½ pound	yellow or red peppers, thinly sliced
4 ounces	button mushrooms, thinly sliced
About 1 pound	tomatoes, peeled, seeded, and diced
1⅓ cups	fish stock (see page 27)

○ Remove and discard any skin from the monkfish and cut flesh into 2-ounce pieces.

○ Marinate the monkfish in the lemon juice with the garlic, herbs, and salt and pepper for 1 to 2 hours.

○ Carefully sauté the onions and peppers in a large nonstick frying pan until just softened.

○ Add the mushrooms and cook for 1 minute, stirring.

○ Add the tomatoes and fish stock and bring to a simmer.

○ Add the drained fish pieces, cover, and simmer for 6 to 8 minutes.

○ Remove the fish and vegetables from the pan and arrange on a suitable dish.

○ Boil the remaining stock rapidly until reduced by half. Pour over the fish and serve immediately.

FILLETS OF HERRING
WITH TOMATOES AND MUSTARD
Filets de hareng aux tomates et moutarde

Herring is becoming more popular again—like sardines—and, prepared
this way, is not only good for the health but also tastes delicious.

SERVES 4

4	herring, about ½ pound each
	Salt and freshly ground pepper
1 teaspoon	herb mustard
1	large, ripe tomato
	Some fresh thyme leaves
3 tablespoons	finely chopped shallots
4 tablespoons	fish stock (see page 27)
	Some fresh tarragon for garnish

○ Gut the herring, cut off the fins, and carefully remove the bone from the head downward. Cut off heads. Remove the skin and take out remaining bones.

○ Wash the fillets and dry well. Season with salt and pepper and rub the mustard on the inside of each fillet. Set aside in a cool place for about 30 minutes.

○ Peel the tomato, quarter it, and remove the core and seeds. Cut the flesh into ½-inch cubes.

○ Place the herring fillets in a nonstick frying pan, sprinkle with thyme leaves, and sauté on both sides until golden brown, about 2 minutes on each side. Remove and keep warm.

○ Sauté the shallots in the same pan until soft, then add the tomato cubes and stock. Season and heat gently.

○ Divide the tomato mixture among four warm plates and arrange the herring fillets on top. Garnish with fresh tarragon and serve immediately.

GRILLED FILLET OF TURBOT
WITH CRAB
Médaillons de turbot, rêve du pécheur

SERVES 4

4	fillets of turbot, about 5 ounces each, skinned
	Salt and freshly ground pepper
3 tablespoons	finely chopped shallots
2 tablespoons	fresh whole wheat bread crumbs
2 ounces	white crab meat
2 teaspoons	freshly cut dill
	A little fish stock (see page 27)
2	medium zucchini, finely diced
3	tomatoes, seeded and diced

○ Season the fillets of turbot with salt and pepper, then grill for 2 minutes on each side.

○ Sauté the shallots in a nonstick pan, stirring, until transparent.

○ Add the bread crumbs, crab meat, and dill and moisten with a little fish stock.

○ Place this mixture on top of the turbot fillets and grill for about 5 minutes longer until the mixture is golden brown.

○ Blanch the zucchini in boiling salted water, drain, and mix with the tomato dice.

○ Arrange the fish on four individual plates and serve with the vegetables.

GOUJONS OF TURBOT WITH BASIL
Goujons de faisan de mer au basilic

SERVES 4

About 1¼ pounds	fillet of turbot, skinned and boned, cut into strips about ½ ounce each
	Salt and finely ground pepper
½ teaspoon	finely chopped orange zest, blanched
⅔ cup	fish stock (see page 27)
2½ tablespoons	finely chopped shallots
About ¼ pound	turnips, peeled, cut into strips, and blanched
8	basil leaves, cut into fine julienne strips
12	orange segments

○ Season the fillets with salt, pepper, and orange zest.

○ Put the fish stock and shallots in a suitable casserole.

○ Add the goujons of turbot, cover, and poach carefully for about 2 minutes.

○ Remove the fish and keep warm. Reduce the stock by one-third.

○ Add the turnips and basil to the stock and season to taste. Simmer for about 30 seconds—the turnips should still be crunchy.

○ Remove a little stock, and in it gently warm the orange segments in a separate pan.

○ Place the goujons of turbot in a suitable dish with the turnips and basil and cover with the well-seasoned stock.

○ Garnish with the warm orange segments.

FILLETS OF SOLE
WITH GRAPES AND WALNUTS
Délices de sole aux raisins et noix

Extra whole cooked crayfish (body shell removed) can be used as a
garnish as well as the parsley.

SERVES 4

8	fillets of sole, about 3 ounces each
	Salt and freshly ground pepper
4	scallops, cut in half
4	shrimp, shells removed, cut in half
4	crayfish, cooked for 2 minutes and shells removed
20	white Muscat grapes, peeled and seeded
12	halves of sweet walnuts, blanched and peeled
	Juice of ½ lemon
½ cup	brown veal stock (see page 22)
1 teaspoon	finely chopped parsley

○ Season the fillets of sole with salt and pepper.

○ Sauté in a nonstick pan for 2 to 3 minutes on each side. Keep warm.

○ Season the scallops, shrimp, and crayfish with salt and pepper.

○ Sauté the scallops, shrimp, and crayfish for 30 seconds. Add the grapes and wal-
nut halves.

○ Place the fillets of sole on a suitable dish and arrange the sautéed seafood, grapes,
and walnuts on top.

○ Add the lemon juice to the hot veal stock, mix in well, then pour carefully around
the fillets of sole.

○ Garnish decoratively with chopped parsley.

FILLETS OF JOHN DORY WITH TOMATO SAUCE
Filets de St. Pierre à la sauce pommes d'amour

Because the tomatoes in the sauce are only heated, not cooked, they retain their vitamins fully.

SERVES 4

2   John Dory fish, weighing about 3 to 3½ pounds in all*
     Salt and freshly ground pepper
8   coriander leaves

Tomato sauce:

About 1 pound   firm, ripe tomatoes, blanched and skinned
4 teaspoons   reduced vegetable stock (see page 26)
1 teaspoon   Dijon mustard
1   small clove of garlic, peeled and crushed
1 teaspoon   *each* of chopped parsley and finely cut tarragon,
                 coriander leaves, and chervil
                 Salt and freshly ground pepper

○ To make the sauce, halve the tomatoes crosswise, remove the seeds, and chop the flesh into tiny dice.

○ Mix together the reduced stock, mustard, garlic, and herbs. Stir in the tomato dice and season to taste with salt and pepper.

○ Wash the fish thoroughly and, using a filleting knife, carefully remove the fillets.

○ Skin the fillets and trim well.

○ Season with salt and pepper, then steam for 3 to 4 minutes.

○ Heat the sauce very gently in a bowl over hot water.

○ Put the slightly warm sauce on four individual plates. Arrange the fillets of fish

on top and serve immediately. Garnish with coriander leaves.

*If John Dory is not available, flounder may be substituted.

STEWED EELS WITH GARLIC
Anguilles à l'ail

SERVES 4

1½ pound	eel, skinned
3 tablespoons	finely chopped shallots
1	clove of garlic, peeled and crushed
¾ cup	fish stock (see page 27)
	Bouquet garni (leek, celery, thyme, parsley stems, and onion, tied together)
12	small white onions
1	medium tomato, peeled, seeded, and diced
8	button mushrooms, well washed and dried
2 tablespoons	chopped parsley
	Dash of lemon juice
	Salt and freshly ground pepper

○ Cut the skinned eel into bite-sized pieces.

○ Sweat the shallots in a nonstick pan without browning for about 2 minutes.

○ Add the pieces of eel and sweat for a further 2 minutes, then add the garlic.

○ Add the fish stock, bouquet garni, and onions. Cover and simmer for 7 to 8 minutes.

○ Add the tomato dice, mushrooms, and parsley. Simmer for 1 to 2 minutes.

○ Season to taste with lemon juice, salt, and pepper. Serve immediately.

FILLET OF TURBOT WITH YELLOW PEPPER SAUCE AND BASIL

Turbot gratinée au basilic, sauce poivrons jaunes

SERVES 4

4	fillets of turbot, about 5 ounces each, boned and skinned
	Few drops lemon juice
	Salt and pepper
¾ cup	fish stock (see page 27)
1	finely chopped shallot
1 cup	fresh breadcrumbs
1 tablespoon	chopped parsley
12	chopped basil leaves
	Yellow pepper sauce to serve
	Basil leaves to garnish

○ Season the turbot fillets with lemon juice, salt, and pepper.

○ Place in a gratin dish with the fish stock and chopped shallot. Bring slowly to the boil and remove from the heat.

○ Mix together the breadcrumbs, parsley, and chopped basil. Season with salt and pepper and sprinkle over the fish.

○ Place under a hot broiler for about 4 minutes until golden.

○ Serve at once with yellow pepper sauce, and garnish with basil leaves.

Yellow pepper sauce:

2	medium yellow peppers
1 tablespoon	finely chopped shallots
1	small clove garlic, whole
	Few sprigs fresh thyme
1½ cups	fish stock (see page 27)
	Pinch sugar

○ Wash and trim the peppers and cut them into large pieces.

○ Sweat the shallots and garlic in a nonstick pan over gentle heat, without browning. Add the yellow peppers and thyme.

○ Add the fish stock and simmer for 15 minutes.

○ Liquidize in a blender and season with sugar, salt, and pepper to taste.

SHELLFISH

Shellfish are divided into many groups. For example, there are bivalve mollusks, which are invertebrates with a hinged shell (mussels, oysters, and scallops). Crustaceans have a protective external skeleton, a jointed "shell" (lobsters, crabs, and shrimp). Like fish in general, and white fish in particular, shellfish of all varieties are packed with protein, vitamins, and minerals and are low in fat. Shellfish are used frequently in Cuisine Naturelle recipes, many having already appeared in the Soups and Appetizers sections. Shellfish are best if prepared as simply as possible, are light, nutritious, and delicious to eat, and are ideal for Cuisine Naturelle cooking.

Remember to try a little fish herb mixture (see page 36) instead of some of the salt in the following recipes.

Crayfish *Écrevisse*

This small freshwater crustacean should always be cooked live, in boiling court bouillon. It is common practice to devein crayfish before cooking, and this step is essential for the flavor. Please note:
1. The cooking liquid should always be ready and boiling.
2. Work in small batches.
3. Hold the crayfish by the carapace, twist the middle section of the end of the tail by pulling carefully, then draw out the fragile blue thread.
4. Cook the crayfish immediately.

Lobster *Homard*

Among the largest crustaceans and the best in flavor are female lobsters (males are less tasty because they run too much, do not feed properly, and exhaust themselves with their love affairs!). Not only does the female have a delicate strip of meat in the head, lacking in the male, but when pregnant has the tasty roe or coral under the tail (a female lobster can be identified by the wider shell underneath, to accommodate the roe). Lobster roe should always be kept, cooked separately, and used for garnish. The ideal weight is 1¾ to 2 pounds. Lobsters should be cooked live; always choose one that is lively and heavy for its size, with a hard shell. The tail should spring back when straightened out.

Mussels *Moules*

This familiar bivalve is found around the world's coasts and is rich in minerals like iron and iodine—required by the body in small amounts but essential for health. If you collect your own mussels, always make sure that the water is unpolluted; if buying, discard any with broken shells or which are open and do not close immediately when tapped. To clean thoroughly before cooking, place in clean water with a little salt for a couple of hours. Before cooking, the shells must be scraped, scrubbed, and well washed to get rid of sand. Mussels are always cooked live; any that have not opened after a few minutes' cooking should be discarded.

Oysters *Huîtres*

The biggest are by no means the best, and a variety of sizes and shapes come from all over the world—the best known from France, Portugal, the Mediterranean, the American Atlantic coast, and the Essex and Kentish beds of Britain. The best are considered to be Belons from the river of the same name in Finistère. Oysters for eating raw and for cooking should be alive and fresh; for eating raw, they should be opened a maximum of 15 minutes before.

Shrimp *Crevettes*

These crustaceans come in a multitude of colors and sizes.

Scallops *Coquilles St. Jacques*

These are bivalves, and there are many species in many seas. Sea scallops may be as large as three inches in diameter. The more expensive bay scallops are usually less than one inch in diameter. Use them as soon as possible.

MARINATED SCALLOPS SUSAN HAMPSHIRE

Noix de coquilles St. Jacques, Susan Hampshire

This dish—created especially for my good friend Susan Hampshire—relies very much on the visual effect of the mounds of vegetables surrounding the scallops. The vegetables must all be cut into *very* fine julienne strips.

SERVES 4

32	sea scallops
	Juice of 1 lime
1	thin slice fresh ginger, peeled and cut into very fine julienne strips
1 tablespoon	finely cut fresh coriander leaves
	Salt and freshly ground pepper
2	carrots, peeled
2	stalks of celery, trimmed
1	medium zucchini
1	red pepper, cored and seeded
⅛ pound	snowpeas, trimmed
6 to 8	radishes, trimmed
⅝ cup	low-fat natural yogurt (see page 31)
1 to 1½ tablespoons	lobster coral (optional)
1 teaspoon	vinegar (optional)

○ Cut the scallops horizontally into circles with a sharp knife.

○ Lay the scallops on a plate and sprinkle with lime juice, ginger, and cut coriander. Season with salt and pepper and let marinate for 5 minutes.

○ Meanwhile, cut each vegetable separately into fine julienne strips. Add a little yogurt to each vegetable mound, season well, and mix in thoroughly.

○ If using it, place lobster coral in a saucepan with a minimum of water, 1 teaspoon vinegar, and a pinch of salt. Bring to the boil, drain, and cool quickly in ice water.

○ Place marinated scallop slices in the center of each of four individual plates. Decorate the outside of each plate with mounds of the different vegetables and the lobster coral. Serve immediately.

SCALLOPS WITH TOMATOES AND BASIL

Coquilles St. Jacques aux tomates et basilic

SERVES 4

16	sea scallops
1 tablespoon	finely chopped shallots
1⅓ cups	fish stock (see page 27)
	A pinch of saffron strands
2 tablespoons	fromage blanc (see page 29)
3	large tomatoes, peeled, seeded, and diced
1 tablespoon	basil, cut into very fine julienne strips
	Salt and freshly ground pepper
8	basil leaves to garnish

○ Halve the scallops and lay on a cloth to dry.

○ Sweat the finely chopped shallots in a nonstick pan without letting them brown.

○ Pour in the fish stock and allow to simmer for 2 minutes. Add the scallops and simmer for 15 seconds.

○ Remove the scallops from the stock and keep them warm.

○ Bring the stock to the boil, add the saffron, and simmer for 5 minutes. Stir in the fromage blanc and warm gently without boiling.

○ Add two-thirds of the tomatoes with the cut basil and season to taste.

○ Spoon the sauce onto four individual plates and arrange the scallops on top. Garnish with the reserved tomato dice and the basil leaves.

CASSEROLE OF MUSSELS WITH FENNEL
Cassolette de moules parfumées au fenouil

This is a very honest way of producing a mussel recipe. Mussels taste very good with the fennel, but you could also use curry spices, saffron, or other flavorings.

SERVES 4

4½ pounds	mussels, scrubbed, brushed, and beards removed
2½ cups	water
1 tablespoon	finely chopped shallot
1 tablespoon	diced celery
⅔ cup	finely cut fennel
	A few parsley stems
	A little thyme
1	small carrot, cut into fine julienne strips
½	small leek, cut into fine julienne strips
	Salt, freshly ground pepper, and cayenne
8	fennel leaves for garnish

○ Discard any mussels that float during the cleaning or that refuse to close when tapped sharply with a knife. Wash thoroughly.

○ Bring the water, shallot, celery, half the fennel, the parsley, and thyme to the boil in a wide, shallow pan.

○ Add the mussels in one layer, season with pepper, cover, and bring to the boil again. Boil only until the mussels open—about 3 to 4 minutes—or they will become tough. Discard any that have not opened.

○ Remove the mussels from the stock with a skimming ladle. Strain the stock carefully through cheesecloth (to get rid of any sand) and then reduce by boiling to about 1 cup.

○ Meanwhile, take the mussels out of their shells, remove and discard any remaining beards and dark "elastic bands," and keep the mussels warm.

○ Sauté the rest of the fennel with the carrot and leek julienne in a nonstick pan for about 2 minutes, stirring constantly.

○ Add the vegetables and shelled mussels to the reduced hot stock and season to taste.

○ Serve in individual bowls or soup plates and garnish with fennel leaves.

POACHED OYSTERS
WRAPPED IN LETTUCE LEAVES
Huîtres en feuilles vertes

Oysters—renowned more for their supposed aphrodisiac properties than for their protein content—are wrapped in lettuce leaves for an unusual and attractive dish.

SERVES 4

24	small lettuce leaves
24	oysters
1 cup	fish stock (see page 27)
1 tablespoon	finely chopped shallots
2 tablespoons	*each* of fine julienne of carrot, leek, and celery
	A dash of lemon juice
	Salt and freshly ground pepper

○ Plunge the lettuce leaves into boiling water. Return to the boil, then remove at once to ice-cold water. Drain well and remove any coarse ribs.

○ Open the oysters with an oyster knife or small strong knife. Strain the liquid into the fish stock and reserve.

○ Remove oysters from the shells and cut away the tendon. Season with pepper.

○ Wrap each oyster in a lettuce leaf. Reserve and wash the bottom half of each oyster shell and warm them.

○ Gently sauté the shallots without coloring in a nonstick pan.

○ Add the fish stock with the oyster water, and heat to a gentle simmer. Add the oyster packages and poach for 15 seconds. Remove the oysters and keep warm.

○ Boil stock rapidly for 3 to 4 minutes until reduced by half.

○ Add the carrot, leek, and celery julienne and cook for 1 minute. Season to taste with lemon juice, salt, and pepper.

○ Place an oyster package back in each warmed shell and spoon the sauce over. Serve at once.

JUMBO SHRIMP
WITH ZUCCHINI AND GINGER
Crevettes aux courgettes et gingembre

SERVES 4

12	jumbo shrimp, removed from their shells and deveined (reserve shells for stock)
⅓ cup	scallions
1 teaspoon	chopped fresh ginger
2	medium zucchini, thinly sliced
½	red pepper, peeled and thinly sliced
1 tablespoon	chopped parsley
	A dash of lemon juice
	Salt and cayenne
	Dill sprigs to garnish

Shrimp stock:

1 tablespoon	finely chopped shallots
½	clove of garlic, peeled and chopped
	A few sprigs of parsley
1 cup	water
	Salt and freshly ground pepper

○ Make the shrimp stock by sautéing the shrimp shells in a nonstick pan for 2 minutes. Add the shallots, garlic, and parsley and sauté for 5 minutes.

○ Add the water and bring to the boil, then cover and simmer for 20 minutes. Strain through fine cheesecloth, then season to taste.

○ Sauté the scallions and ginger in a nonstick pan without browning.

○ Add the zucchini and sauté for 1 minute before adding ⅔ cup of the shrimp stock.

○ Add the pepper slices and simmer gently for about 2 to 3 minutes until the stock is reduced slightly.

○ Add the parsley and lemon juice and season to taste with salt and cayenne.

○ Season the raw jumbo shrimp with salt and cayenne and poach in the remaining stock for 2 to 3 minutes. Remove and add the stock to the sauce.

○ Arrange the vegetables and sauce on four individual plates. Place the shrimp on top and garnish with dill sprigs.

CRAYFISH RAGOUT
WITH GREEN ASPARAGUS
Ragoût d'écrevisses et d'asperges vertes

SERVES 4

36	live crayfish
16	green asparagus spears, trimmed and peeled
1 tablespoon	finely chopped shallots
1¼ cups	crayfish stock (see below)
	Salt and freshly ground pepper
12	very small new carrots, peeled and blanched
4	sprigs of chervil to garnish

○ Cook the crayfish in boiling salted water for 1 minute (see page 123). Remove from the water and place in a bowl of ice to cool quickly.

○ Remove the tails from the shells and reserve body and tail shells to make stock (follow method for shrimp stock in following recipe). Keep the tails fresh (cover with a damp cloth).

○ Cook the asparagus in lightly salted water until just tender, about 3 minutes.

○ Sauté the shallots gently, without browning, until transparent, stirring constantly.

○ Add the crayfish stock and bring to the boil. Continue boiling until reduced by half.

○ Strain into a clean saucepan, adjust seasoning, then add the crayfish, asparagus, and carrots and heat carefully without boiling.

○ Arrange in individual soup plates and garnish with sprigs of chervil.

A SYMPHONY OF SEAFOOD
Symphonie de fruits de mer

This can be served as either an appetizer or a main course. (As an appetizer, it will serve 6 to 8 people.)

SERVES 4

8	sea scallops in their shells
12	fresh mussels in their shells
8	tiny squid
5 ounces	fillet of turbot, skinned and cut into cubes about ½ ounce each
12	medium shrimp, removed from their shells
8	jumbo shrimp, removed from their shells and deveined
	Cayenne, salt, and freshly ground pepper
1	leek, white part mainly
1¾ cups	fish stock (see page 27)
4	sprigs of fresh thyme

○ Wash scallops briefly but thoroughly.

○ Cut each scallop in half horizontally and lay on a damp cloth.

○ Scrub the mussel shells and remove the beard. Place in a saucepan and heat gently until the mussels open. Discard any that remain closed.

○ Remove the tentacles from the squid (reserve the bodies for another dish). Wash well and blanch in boiling water for 30 seconds. Drain and cool.

○ Season the turbot and shrimps with cayenne, salt, and pepper.

○ Thinly slice the leek and blanch in boiling salted water. Drain and cool.

○ Heat the fish stock to a gentle simmer, add the squid and jumbo shrimp, and poach for 1 minute.

○ Add the medium shrimp and turbot and poach for 1 minute.

○ Add the leek and mussels and poach for a further 30 seconds.

○ Add the scallops and thyme and poach for yet another 30 seconds.

○ Carefully arrange the fish in four individual soup dishes.

○ Check the seasoning of the stock and adjust to taste. Bring just to serving temperature, then pour over the fish and serve at once.

GRILLED SEAFOOD SAUSAGES WITH CARROT LEAF SAUCE
Boudins de fruits de mer, sauce aux feuilles de carottes

Sausage casings are now easily available, but if they are too firm, remove them carefully from the sausages before grilling—the poaching will have set the filling in shape. When carrot tops are not available for the sauce, use a mixture of green leaves and herbs such as watercress, sorrel, and parsley. This dish can be served either as an appetizer or a main course: halve quantities for the former; add a nice accompaniment for the latter.

SERVES 4

4	scallops
4	jumbo shrimp, removed from their shells and deveined
5 ounces	fillet of salmon, skinned, boned, and cut into small cubes
4 ounces	fillet of monkfish, skinned and cut into small cubes
	Salt and freshly ground pepper
7 ounces	fillet of whiting or pike, skinned and boned
1	egg white
½ cup	fromage blanc (see page 29)
2 tablespoons	finely cut dill
16- to 20-inch	sausage casing, soaked in water

Sauce:

About ¾ pound	carrot tops, washed
⅞ cup	fish stock (see page 27)
1⅜ cups	fromage blanc (see page 29)
	Salt and freshly ground pepper

○ Cut the scallops into small pieces and lay on a cloth to dry.

○ Season the scallops, jumbo shrimp, salmon, and monkfish with salt and pepper.

○ Purée the whiting or pike in a food processor. Add the egg white and a pinch of salt and pepper and process until smooth.

○ Place the puréed fish mixture in a bowl over ice. Gradually beat in fromage blanc.

○ Add all the seasoned fish and the cut dill. Season and let rest for 30 to 40 minutes. The consistency should be like that of choux dough.

○ To make the sauce, retain four carrot sprigs for garnish, then blanch the remainder in the fish stock for about 1 minute. Drain, dip in cold water, then drain again.

○ Purée the carrot tops in a food processor or blender, adding some of the liquid if necessary. Strain.

○ Reduce the remaining fish stock by half by rapid boiling.

○ Add the fromage blanc and the purée to the reduced stock and mix until smooth. Bring to the boil and season.

○ Fill the sausage casing with the fish mixture, using a pastry bag or spoon and shape into four "sausages" about 4 inches long. Bind the ends of each sausage with string.

○ Poach them in hot water (do not boil) for 5 to 6 minutes. Drain and cool in cold water. (The casing can now be removed if desired.)

○ Grill under medium heat for 5 to 6 minutes, turning occasionally, until golden brown.

○ Spoon the warm sauce onto four plates and place the sausages on top. Garnish each plate with a small piece of carrot top.

LOBSTER WITH TOMATO AND WATERCRESS
Homard à la tomate et au cresson

With the technique outlined below, the lobster stays tender and moist,
and the sautéing gives extra flavor.

SERVES 4

4	live female lobsters, about ¾ pound each
3 quarts	court bouillon (see page 28)
8	basil leaves, finely cut
1 quantity	of tomato coulis (see page 141)

Watercress purée:

About 1 pound	watercress, *or* ½ pound trimmed watercress leaves
5 cups	water
	Juice of ½ lemon
1½ ounces	tofu
	Salt and freshly ground pepper

○ Splash the live lobsters with cold water, then plunge them into the boiling court bouillon for 2 minutes.

○ Remove the pan from the heat, but leave the lobsters in the court bouillon. Place the pan in a large bowl of ice to cool quickly.

○ Meanwhile, make the watercress purée and the tomato coulis.

○ For the purée, remove the larger stems from the watercress and blanch the leaves in the 5 cups of boiling salted water for about 1 minute.

○ Drain the watercress, then plunge immediately into ice water to hold the color and stop the cooking process. Drain again and dry on paper towels.

○ Purée in a food processor or blender with the lemon juice and tofu.

○ Warm the sauce in a double boiler, stirring occasionally. Check seasoning, and add salt and pepper if necessary.

○ When the lobster is cold, remove the tails and cut through the shell underneath with scissors. Remove and carefully shell the claws, discarding the cartilage.

○ Cut the tail into medallions about ¼ inch thick and cut the claws in half.

○ Place the lobster meat in a hot nonstick pan and add the basil leaves. Sauté for 5 seconds on each side.

○ Pour the tomato coulis onto four individual plates. Arrange the lobster medallions, claw meat, and basil on top and spoon a little warm watercress purée over them.

SAUTEED SCALLOPS WITH LEEK PUREE
Coquilles St. Jacques à la purée de poireaux

SERVES 4

3	medium leeks, trimmed, tender green part only
6 tablespoons	fish stock (see page 27)
¼ cup	fromage blanc (see page 29)
	Salt and freshly ground pepper
24	sea scallops
4	fresh basil leaves to garnish

○ Cut the leeks into pieces and wash very well.

○ Cook the leeks in the stock until tender, about 5 minutes. Purée in a blender or food processor, then stir in the fromage blanc and season with salt and pepper to taste.

○ Cut the scallops in half and sauté them in a nonstick pan for about 5 seconds on each side.

○ Spoon the leek purée onto individual plates. Arrange the scallops on top, then garnish each plate with some coral and a basil leaf.

GLAZED OYSTERS ON A BED OF CRAB
Huîtres et crabe des isles gratinées

SERVES 4

24	oysters
	Juice of ½ lemon
4 tablespoons	fish stock (see page 27)
1	egg yolk
	Salt and freshly ground pepper
3 ounces	white crab meat
	Lemon crown and tomato rose to garnish

○ Open the oysters and cut away the silver tendon that holds the oyster to the shell. Remove the oysters from their shells. Strain any liquid into a small pan.

○ Place oysters in the pan, add the lemon juice and stock, and poach for 15 seconds.

○ Remove from the pan and reduce the stock by half by rapid boiling.

○ Remove from heat and whisk in egg yolk. Season to taste with a little salt and pepper.

○ Wash the bottom half of each oyster shell and place a little warmed crab meat in each.

○ Place the oysters on top and coat with the sauce. Place under a hot broiler for about 30 seconds until golden.

○ Serve at once on a dish garnished with a lemon crown and tomato rose.

TOMATO COULIS
Sauce coulis de tomates

This is a pure sauce, colorful and tasty, which can be used for many other Cuisine Naturelle recipes. Finely chopped tomatoes can be added to the sauce as a garnish.

SERVES 4

1¼ pounds	firm, ripe tomatoes, skinned and seeded
¼ cup	finely chopped shallots
½	clove of garlic, peeled and crushed
2	sprigs of fresh thyme
2	sprigs of fresh rosemary
4 tablespoons	reduced vegetable stock (see page 26)
	Salt and freshly ground pepper

○ Make sure all seeds, skin, and excess juice have been eliminated from the tomatoes.

○ Sauté the shallots and garlic in a nonstick pan for 3 to 4 minutes, stirring constantly.

○ Add the herbs and sautée for about 1 minute, very gently.

○ Add the tomatoes and vegetable stock and simmer for 10 to 12 minutes.

○ Remove the herbs and purée the sauce in a blender.

○ Pour the sauce back into the saucepan, bring to the boil, and season with salt and pepper.

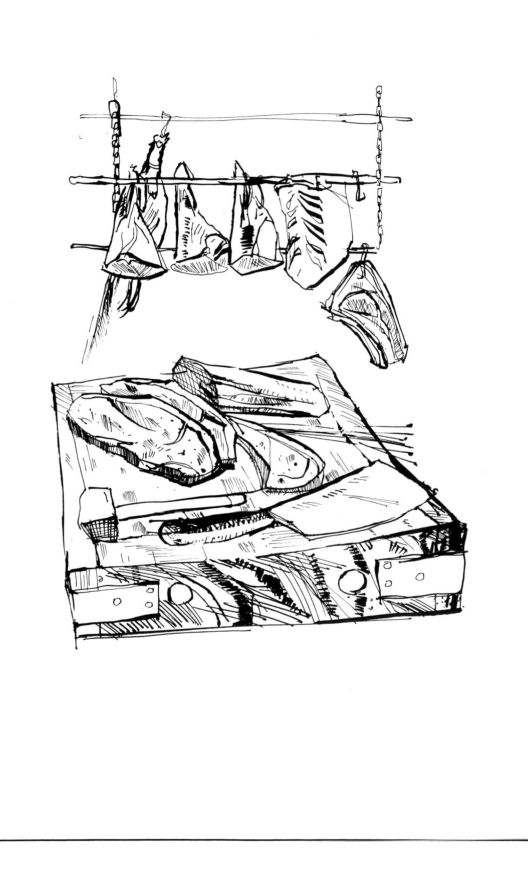

MEAT

Meat is full of protein but also contains hidden fat. It is, of course, this hidden fat that moistens the meat and gives it its flavor—and Cuisine Naturelle would not wish to deny anyone the undoubted pleasures of a good, tender slice of meat. The Cuisine Naturelle solution is, as in all the other recipes, to prepare without butter, cream, or oil—any *added* fat—or alcohol. The meats selected are the leanest possible, all obvious fat is cut away carefully, and the chosen sauces and accompaniments are natural, complementing, flavoring, and moistening. The quantity of meat served has been reduced as well, to create a better balance—people are tending to eat less meat these days anyway.

Good meat needs to be cut carefully, not haphazardly. Connective tissues lying between the muscles make it easier to separate the various parts; thus subcutaneous layers of fat and sinew can be removed without much difficulty, leaving the compact muscles. The most tender meat comes from the parts of the animals that have "moved" least, the muscles being tougher at leg, neck, and shoulder.

Meat should always be kept dry, away from steam and products that produce steam, because it becomes sticky with damp.

Variety meats—liver, kidney, sweetbreads, and tongue—are usually the healthiest parts of the animal to eat. They are comparatively low in fat, and most contain a high proportion of vitamins and minerals—liver, for instance, is rich in vitamins A and B and iron.

To cut down on the use of salt in the following recipes, use some of the herb mixture for meat on page 36.

Beef *Boeuf*

Young first-class beef should be red in color but not too dark. A marbled effect in the meat—of fat running through the tissue—is a sign of proper fattening, and of the breed of the animal, and will guarantee its tenderness. Beef should be hung for about 15 to 21 days before use.

Veal *Veau*

A properly fattened, milk-fed calf will have a pinkish-white flesh, and the kidney should be completely covered in white fat. Meat from calves that are too young, or that have not been fattened properly, will disintegrate during preparation. Veal should be hung for 8 to 10 days before use.

Lamb *Agneau*

Most chefs prefer lamb to beef and pork because it is more tender, with a pronounced taste of its own. Lamb should always be prepared as simply as possible to preserve that special taste. The best meat comes from grazing sheep that are not yet fully grown—about ten months old. Milk-fed lambs—available only in spring—are animals that are still suckling and not yet grazing; they have white flesh. Lamb, like all other kinds of meat, should be hung for a few days before use.

Pork *Porc*

Good pork is pale pink in color and slightly marbled. It should never be dark red or watery. It should be hung for 5 to 6 days before use.

BEEF SIRLOIN, DANNY KAYE
Entrecôte double de boeuf, Danny Kaye

This recipe was first prepared for Danny Kaye, who is not only a world-famous actor but also an extremely good cook. Some of my happiest hours have been spent in his company.
Serve the almost raw beef slices with Meaux mustard or a mustard sauce passed separately.

SERVES 4

1½ pounds	beef sirloin steak in one piece, boned and well trimmed of fat
	Salt
2 tablespoons	black peppercorns, crushed
1 tablespoon	red wine vinegar
1 teaspoon	soy sauce
1 teaspoon	*each* of chopped shallot and finely cut chives
½ teaspoon	*each* of chopped tarragon and finely cut parsley and garlic
	Freshly ground pepper
3	egg whites
	Watercress leaves to garnish

○ Rub the sirloin with peppercorns and salt.

○ In a nonstick frying pan—or directly on a griddle—brown and sear the sirloin, about 2 minutes on each side.

○ Whisk together the vinegar, soy sauce, shallot, chives, tarragon, parsley, and garlic until well blended and thick. Season with salt and pepper to taste.

○ Whisk egg whites until frothy, then add dressing and whisk again.

○ Thinly slice the steak, arrange on a plate or on individual plates, and spoon the sauce over. Serve immediately, garnished with watercress.

FILLET OF BEEF
WITH ROSEMARY AND MUSTARD
Rosette de boeuf gratiné au romarin

Garnish the steaks with vegetables of choice, perhaps leaf spinach with
toasted croutons, new carrots, and Jacqueline potatoes.

SERVES 4

4	fillet steaks, about 5 ounces each, well trimmed of fat
	Salt and freshly ground pepper
2½ teaspoons	finely chopped shallots
1 teaspoon	finely chopped garlic
1¾ cups	brown veal stock (see page 22)
1½ cups	fresh bread crumbs
2 teaspoons	freshly chopped parsley
2 teaspoons	freshly chopped rosemary
	Juice of ½ lemon
2 teaspoons	English (strong) mustard

○ Season the fillets with salt and pepper.

○ Sauté in a hot nonstick pan for about 2 minutes on each side. Remove from the
pan and keep warm.

○ Add the shallots and garlic to the pan and sauté at a lower temperature, stirring
constantly, until transparent.

○ Add the brown veal stock and reduce by half by rapid boiling.

○ In the meantime, mix the bread crumbs and herbs together. Add the lemon juice.

○ Brush the mustard on top of each fillet.

○ Top with the herb mixture and put the fillets under a hot grill until golden brown
(about 1 to 2 minutes).

○ Put the well-seasoned sauce and meat on a plate and garnish with vegetables of
choice.

FILETS MIGNONS
WITH SHALLOT SAUCE
Mignons de boeuf sautés aux échalotes

Filet mignon is also known as fillet steak and is a small cut from the fillet. It is lean and tender and should be handled with great care and love.

SERVES 4

8	filets mignons, well trimmed, 2 to 3 ounces each
	Salt and freshly ground pepper
¼ cup	finely chopped shallots
1⅓ cups	brown veal stock (see page 22)
2 teaspoons	lemon juice

○ Season the well-trimmed steaks with salt and pepper.

○ Sauté them on both sides in a nonstick pan for 3 to 4 minutes. Remove and keep warm.

○ Add the chopped shallots to the pan and sauté without browning.

○ Add the brown veal stock and reduce by rapid boiling to half its original volume.

○ Season with salt, pepper, and lemon juice.

○ Coat the steaks with the sauce and serve immediately.

GRILLED RIB STEAK
WITH GARDEN HERBS
Côte de boeuf grillée aux herbes du jardin

To prevent the meat juices from escaping, the beef should rest for 10
minutes before being cut. Serve with Carrot and Spinach Mousse.
The wing rib, closest to the sirloin, is recommended for this recipe.

SERVES 4

2¾ pounds	rib steak, with bone, and trimmed well of fat
1	small sprig of thyme
1	small sprig of rosemary
4	sage leaves, finely cut
1	clove of garlic, crushed
	Salt and coarsely ground black pepper
1	bunch of watercress, well washed and trimmed, for garnish

○ Using a rolling pin or a mallet, flatten the beef to the depth of the rib bone.

○ Place in a shallow dish.

○ Finely chop all the herbs and mix with the garlic.

○ Press the herbs into both sides of the meat and leave covered in a cool place for 2 to 3 hours.

○ Season with salt and pepper.

○ Grill under medium heat for 10 to 12 minutes, turning once during this time.

○ Serve in slices garnished with watercress sprigs.

POACHED SADDLE OF LAMB
Selle d'agneau pochée à la paysanne

To give this dish a special taste, poach an unpeeled clove of garlic in the stock along with the lamb and vegetables. Because the garlic is not crushed, the flavor is much more subtle.

SERVES 4

About 1¼ pounds	saddle of lamb, boned and well trimmed of fat
1⅓ cups	white veal stock (see page 20)
1⅓ cups	lamb stock (see page 23)
2	onions, 1 red and 1 white, peeled, quartered, and broken up
2	medium leeks, white part only, cut into diagonal slices
1¾ cups	roughly chopped savoy cabbage leaves
¼ pound	small brussels sprouts, divided into individual leaves
	A little finely chopped parsley and finely cut chives and basil
	Salt and freshly ground pepper

○ Skin and trim the lamb. Cut into four pieces.

○ Pour the veal and lamb stocks into a saucepan and reduce by boiling by one-quarter.

○ Quickly blanch the onions, leeks, cabbage, and brussels sprouts in boiling salted water. Remove and allow to drain.

○ Add the pieces of lamb to the reduced stock and allow to simmer for 2 to 3 minutes.

○ Add the blanched vegetables to the stock and simmer for 2 to 3 minutes.

○ Add the freshly chopped parsley, cut chives and basil, and season with salt and pepper.

○ Remove the vegetables and arrange in a suitable dish.

○ Just before serving, cut the meat into pieces slightly less than ½ inch thick and arrange on the vegetables. Serve immediately.

LOIN OF LAMB
WITH THYME AND SPINACH
Longe d'agneau au thym et épinards

A mousse of broccoli may be served if tender young spinach is not available.

SERVES 4

2	loins of lamb, about 1¼ pounds total, after boning and trimming well of fat
	Salt and freshly ground pepper
4 tablespoons	finely chopped shallots
1	clove of garlic, finely chopped
3 tablespoons	fresh thyme sprigs
1¾ cups	lamb stock (see page 23)
¾ pound	spinach leaves, stems removed, roughly chopped, blanched, and well drained
¼ cup	fromage blanc (see page 29)
16	tiny sprigs of thyme for garnish
4	small tomatoes, peeled and seeded, then each cut into 4 diamond shapes, for garnish

○ Season the loins of lamb with salt and pepper, then sauté them in a nonstick pan for about 6 to 7 minutes, turning once. Remove from the pan and keep warm.

○ Add half the shallots, with the garlic and thyme, to the pan and sauté, stirring all the time, until the shallots are transparent.

○ Add the lamb stock and reduce by boiling to half the quantity. Strain and season to taste. Keep the sauce warm.

○ Sauté the remaining shallots in a nonstick pan.

○ Add the spinach leaves and sauté for about 2 minutes.

○ Add the fromage blanc, mix well, and season to taste.

○ Press the spinach mixture into four small ramekins and allow to set for 30 seconds.

○ Place a tiny sprig of thyme onto each tomato diamond and place in a warm oven (about 300° F) until warmed through.

○ Spoon a little sauce into the center of each of four plates. Unmold the spinach onto the center of each plate.

○ Slice each piece of lamb into eight pieces. Arrange four slices around each spinach mold.

○ Garnish with the tomato diamonds and serve at once.

SAUTEED MEDALLIONS OF VEAL WITH FRESH MARKET VEGETABLES
Mignons de veau aux légumes du marché

Any vegetables can be used in this recipe, according to the season. After blanching, cool the vegetables quickly in cold vegetable stock, over ice.

SERVES 4

8	medallions of veal, about 2½ ounces each, well trimmed of all fat
	Salt and freshly ground pepper
⅛ pound	small snowpeas, blanched for 10 seconds
2	medium carrots, cut in strips and blanched for 20 seconds
¼ pound	salsify, cut in strips and blanched for 20 seconds
⅛ pound	green beans, cut in half and blanched for 10 seconds
⅞ cup	fromage blanc (see page 29)
⅝ cup	low-fat natural yogurt (see page 31)
2 tablespoons	finely cut chives

○ Season the veal medallions with salt and pepper.

○ Sauté in a hot nonstick pan on each side for about 2 to 3 minutes, until still pink. Remove from pan and keep warm.

○ Dry the vegetables on paper towels, then sauté them in the same pan for about 1 minute. Season with salt and pepper.

○ Meanwhile, whisk together the fromage blanc and yogurt and heat gently, whisking continually until light and frothy.

○ Season to taste with chives, salt, and pepper.

○ Pour sauce onto four individual serving plates, garnish with the vegetables, and place the meat on top.

COLD LOIN OF VEAL
WITH BASIL SAUCE
Longe de veau froide au basilic

Turkey or breast of chicken can be prepared in this way as well. The sauce may be enhanced with small cubes of red pepper.

SERVES 4

About 1¼ pounds	loin of veal, bone and excess fat removed
2	medium carrots, peeled and diced
⅛ pound	celeriac, peeled and diced
1	clove of garlic, unpeeled
1	small bay leaf
½	clove
1	medium onion, peeled and cut in half
2 cups	white veal stock (see page 20)
	Salt and freshly ground pepper
2 teaspoons	freshly cut basil
1 tablespoon	freshly chopped parsley
⅝ cup	fromage blanc (see page 29)
	Juice of ½ lemon
1	tomato, peeled, seeded, and diced

○ Simmer the meat in a nonstick pan together with the carrots, celeriac, garlic clove, bay leaf, clove, onion, and veal stock, seasoned with salt and pepper, for 30 minutes until just cooked.

○ Allow to cool in the stock.

○ Reduce 1 cup of the stock to just less than half its volume and put to one side for the sauce.

○ Put half the basil, with all the parsley, the reduced stock, and the vegetables and skinned soft garlic clove into a food processor or blender and purée.

○ Add the fromage blanc and mix in well, then season with salt, pepper, and lemon juice.

○ Very thinly slice the veal and arrange in a ring on a serving dish or on individual plates.

○ Cover with the well-seasoned sauce and sprinkle with the remaining basil.

○ Arrange tomato dice attractively in the middle of the dish or plate.

STEAMED CALF'S SWEETBREADS
Ris de veau à la vapeur

SERVES 4

1¼ pounds	calf's sweetbreads
1⅓ cups	white veal stock, well seasoned (see page 20)
¼ cup	diced onion
3 tablespoons	diced carrot
3 tablespoons	diced leek
3 tablespoons	diced celery
1	small bay leaf
	A few sprigs of parsley
14	basil leaves
	Salt and freshly ground white pepper
2½ ounces	lean cooked ham, cut into thick strips

○ Soak the sweetbreads for several hours in water, changing frequently.

○ Blanch the sweetbreads in boiling salted water for 2 to 3 minutes. Remove the membrane with a small sharp knife.

○ Put the veal stock in a saucepan with the vegetables, bay leaf, sprigs of parsley, and six of the basil leaves.

○ Place a steamer on top and steam the sweetbreads and ham for 5 minutes.

○ Remove the sweetbreads and keep warm.

○ Strain the stock and boil rapidly to reduce to one-third of the original volume. Season with salt and pepper to taste.

○ Spoon the sauce onto a plate and arrange slices of sweetbread on top. Garnish with strips of ham and the remaining basil leaves.

SAUTEED CALF'S LIVER WITH GARLIC
Foie de veau sauté à l'ail

Any other type of liver could be used in this recipe, but calf's is by far
the most tender. The vitamin C of the barely cooked vegetables helps
the assimilation of the iron in the liver.

SERVES 4

1 tablespoon	cornstarch
1 tablespoon	lemon juice
1	egg white
1 tablespoon	soy sauce
1 pound	calf's liver, cut in strips
About ½ pound	snowpeas
6	shallots or small white onions
1 tablespoon	fresh ginger, peeled and chopped
	Generous ½ cup brown veal stock (see page 22)
1	small clove of garlic, crushed
	Freshly ground pepper

○ Mix together 2 teaspoons of the cornstarch, the lemon juice, lightly beaten egg white, and 1 teaspoon of the soy sauce.

○ Mix the liver strips with the marinade and leave for 20 minutes.

○ Wash and trim the snowpeas and peel the shallots or onions.

○ Cut the shallots in half lengthwise and sauté gently in a nonstick pan, turning constantly, for 5 minutes over gentle heat.

○ Add the snowpeas and ginger and, stirring all the time, sauté until half cooked. The vegetables should remain crisp and not lose their color; set aside.

○ Sauté the liver with the marinade in a nonstick pan for 2 to 3 minutes, turning constantly, then remove from the pan.

○ Mix the remaining cornstarch with the remaining soy sauce and the stock. Add to the pan and bring to the boil, stirring all the time, until the sauce is thickened.

○ Mix in the vegetables, add the liver, warm quickly, and season with crushed garlic and a little pepper.

BOILED VEAL TONGUE
WITH CHIVE SAUCE
Langue de veau bouillie à la ciboulette

SERVES 4

1	veal tongue, about 1½ pounds
3 quarts	water
1	medium onion, peeled and sliced
½	bay leaf
1	small leek, trimmed and sliced
1	medium carrot, peeled and sliced
	Salt and freshly ground pepper

Sauce:

4 teaspoons	finely cut chives
½ cup	tongue stock, strained (see below)
1 cup	fromage blanc (see page 29)
	Juice of ½ lemon
	Cayenne
	Salt and freshly ground pepper
8	lengths of chive, about 2 inches long, for garnish

○ Wash the tongue well. Place all the other ingredients for the stock—water, onion, bay leaf, leek, and carrot—in a saucepan. Season with salt and pepper and bring to the boil.

○ Add the tongue and simmer gently for 1½ hours until tender, occasionally removing the fat from the top.

○ Remove the tongue from the stock, allow to cool a little, then peel off the skin with a sharp knife.

○ Reduce 1 cup of the strained stock to half its volume and set aside for the sauce.

○ Remove the fat and any gristly parts from the large end of the tongue.

○ Return the tongue to the strained stock to keep warm.

○ For the sauce, whirl half the cut chives and the ½ cup reduced stock together in a food processor or blender.

○ Mix the fromage blanc and remaining cut chives. Season to taste with lemon juice, cayenne, salt, and pepper. Warm very gently.

○ Remove the tongue from the stock and cut into thin diagonal slices. Arrange on a suitable plate and serve with the sauce, garnished with pieces of chive.

MEDALLIONS OF PORK STUDDED WITH PRUNES
Médaillons de porc piqués aux pruneaux

SERVES 4

12	pork medallions (from the tenderloin), about 2 ounces each, well trimmed of fat
10	pitted prunes, soaked in hot China tea
	Salt and freshly ground pepper
⅔ cup	brown veal stock (see page 22)
About ½ cup	*each* of carrot and turnip julienne
1 tablespoon	chopped parsley to garnish

○ Make two small slits in each piece of pork with a sharp knife.

○ Cut six of the prunes into quarters and press two pieces into each medallion of pork. Season with salt and pepper.

○ Sauté the medallions slowly in a nonstick frying pan for 4 to 5 minutes, turning once. Remove from the pan and keep warm.

○ Add the veal stock to the pan and boil down until reduced to a syrupy glaze. Strain through a sieve, then check the seasoning.

○ Meanwhile, blanch the carrots, turnips, and remaining prunes in boiling water for 30 seconds. Drain and season to taste.

○ Arrange the pork medallions, carrot, turnip, and prunes on a plate.

○ Spoon sauce around the meat and sprinkle with chopped parsley. Serve immediately.

TENDERLOIN OF PORK
WITH CHINESE CABBAGE
Filet de porc à la pékinoise

Ginger and coriander, both very aromatic and believed to aid digestion,
are good accompaniments for this stir-fried dish.

SERVES 4

1 pound	pork tenderloin, well trimmed of fat
	Freshly ground pepper
1	small onion, chopped
1	clove of garlic, crushed
½	small cauliflower, cut into florets
2	large carrots, cut in thin strips
½	bunch of scallions, cut into 1-inch lengths
½	head of Chinese cabbage, cut into 1-inch strips
1 teaspoon	grated fresh ginger
4 tablespoons	white poultry stock (see page 19)
1 tablespoon	soy sauce
	Fresh coriander leaves to garnish

○ Cut the pork tenderloin into thin strips. Season with pepper and sear in a non-stick pan for 2 minutes on each side. Remove from the pan.

○ Sauté the onion, garlic, cauliflower, and carrots for 3 minutes.

○ Add the scallions, Chinese cabbage, ginger, and poultry stock to the pan. Cover and simmer gently for 2 to 3 minutes.

○ Add the pork and season to taste with soy sauce and freshly ground pepper.

○ Serve immediately, garnished with the coriander leaves.

POULTRY

Poultry is the domestic or fattened birds such as chicken, goose, duck, and turkey. All others are classified as game birds. Poultry meat contains protein, vitamins, and minerals (iron and phosphorus), and the meat of young poultry is well known for being easy to digest.

Try to obtain free-range chickens—or the flavorful corn-fed chickens that are widely available now. Baby chickens, or poussins, are the smallest variety, the weight being between 10 and 16 ounces; they are good for grilling. Cornish hens may be substituted when baby chickens are not available.

The majority of the recipes are for chicken, the most popular bird because of its mild, pleasant flavor and its versatility. (Poultry, in fact, is now eaten much more regularly than meat.) It is also the least fatty—and in all the recipes the skin, which does contain fat, is removed. Duck has a fatter meat, but again, with skin removed and served with an acidic accompaniment, it is delicious and easy to digest.

In place of some of the salt in the following recipes, why not use a pinch of the herb mixture for poultry on page 36—this will cut down the need for salt seasoning.

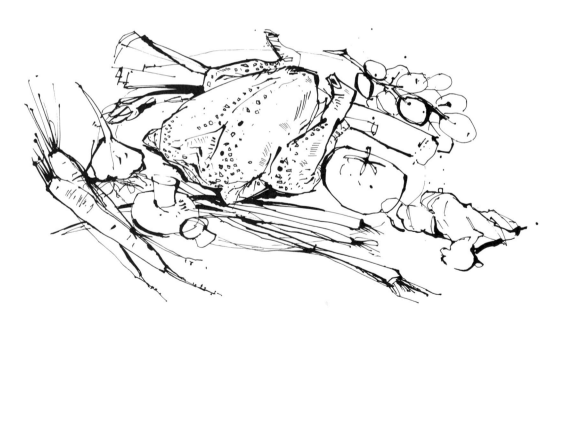

CHICKEN SAUTE WITH FRESH GINGER
Sauté de poulet Mikado

SERVES 4

About 1¼ pounds	chicken meat, skinned, boned, and cut into cubes (both white and dark meat)
	Freshly ground pepper
½	red pepper, seeded and sliced
½	green pepper, seeded and sliced
1	medium carrot, thinly sliced
1	leek, thinly sliced
2 cups	bean sprouts
1-inch piece	fresh ginger (about ¾ ounce) peeled and thinly sliced
2 tablespoons	soy sauce
4 teaspoons	wine vinegar
2 teaspoons	cornstarch
⅞ cup	white poultry stock (see page 19)

○ Season the chicken with pepper and sauté in a nonstick frying pan for about 3 minutes, stirring frequently, until colored on all sides.

○ Remove from the pan and keep warm.

○ Sauté the peppers and carrot for 2 minutes in a nonstick pan.

○ Add the leek and bean sprouts and sauté for 30 to 45 seconds longer.

○ Stir in the ginger, soy sauce, and vinegar.

○ Dissolve the cornstarch in the poultry stock and add to the pan. Add the chicken and stir continuously until it comes to the boil.

○ Season to taste with pepper and serve at once.

BABY CHICKEN WITH GRILLED VEGETABLES
Poussin aux légumes grillés

If you wish, the chicken and vegetables may be marked with a red-hot skewer before grilling to give an attractive finish. This is a version of "quadrillage."
Cornish hens may be substituted if baby chickens are not available.

SERVES 4

4	baby chickens, about ¾ pound each
	Salt and freshly ground pepper
1	large stalk of broccoli (about ½ pound), trimmed and cut into small florets
¼ pound	tiny new carrots, peeled, with some of the green top left on
½ pound	new potatoes, peeled and sliced
2 or 3	tender leeks, cut into 2-inch lengths
2 or 3	baby zucchini, unpeeled and sliced

○ Cut the chickens down the back, press them flat, and remove the backbones and skin. Season with salt and pepper.

○ Blanch the broccoli and carrots in boiling water for 1 minute.

○ Grill the chicken for 10 to 12 minutes under medium heat.

○ Meanwhile, grill all the vegetables under low heat for 5 to 8 minutes until tender.

○ Arrange the chickens on individual serving plates and garnish with the vegetables.

POACHED CHICKEN BREAST WITH RAW SEASONAL VEGETABLES
Blanc de volaille poché aux crudités de saison

A yogurt dressing can be used for the chicken instead of the suggested sauce.

SERVES 4

2	medium carrots, peeled
1	medium zucchini, trimmed
¼ pound	beets, peeled
1	yellow pepper, trimmed
2	stalks of celery, trimmed
¼ pound	radishes, trimmed
4	chicken breasts, about 5 ounces each, skinned and well trimmed
	Salt and freshly ground pepper
2 cups	white poultry stock (see page 19)
4 tablespoons	chives, cut in ½-inch lengths

Sauce:

½ cup	reduced white poultry stock (see below)
2 tablespoons	tarragon vinegar
2 teaspoons	French Dijon-style mustard

○ Cut all the vegetables into very fine julienne strips (or coarsely grate them). Keep each vegetable separate.

○ Season the chicken breasts with salt and pepper, then poach them in the poultry stock for 4 to 5 minutes.

○ Remove the breasts from the stock and cool. Reduce the stock to scant ½ cup, then whisk in the vinegar and mustard to make the sauce.

○ Moisten each pile of vegetables with a little of the sauce, reserving some for the chicken. Season to taste.

○ Arrange small piles of each vegetable around the edge of each plate.

○ Place chicken in the center, spoon over a little of the remaining sauce, and sprinkle with cut chives. Serve immediately.

SAUTE OF CHICKEN WITH MIXED PEPPERS AND HERBS
Sauté de poulet au mélange de piments

To ensure that this dish has a good color, it is important not to overcook
the peppers.

SERVES 4

1	chicken, about 3½ pounds
	Salt and freshly ground pepper
½	medium onion, sliced
1	clove of garlic, finely chopped
¼ pound	mushrooms
1	*each* red, green, and yellow pepper, seeded and cut into quarters
About 1 pound	tomatoes, seeded and diced
2½ cups	brown poultry stock (see page 21)
	A few sprigs of fresh thyme, marjoram, and rosemary, chopped
4	basil leaves, finely cut
	A few sprigs of parsley, chopped, for garnish

○ The chicken should be cut into eight pieces. Remove the skin; season chicken pieces lightly with salt and pepper.

○ Sauté the chicken in a nonstick pan for about 5 minutes. Remove from the pan.

○ Sauté the onion, garlic, mushrooms, and peppers for 1 to 2 minutes, stirring constantly. Transfer to a larger ovenproof pan or dish.

○ Add the tomatoes, chicken pieces, and poultry stock and bring to the boil.

○ Add the thyme, marjoram, rosemary, and basil, cover, and place in a medium oven (375° F) for 10 minutes.

○ Remove the chicken and vegetables, keep warm, and reduce the sauce by rapid boiling. Adjust seasoning.

○ Arrange chicken and vegetables on a suitable dish or dishes. Spoon the sauce over, sprinkle with parsley, and serve.

BREAST OF CHICKEN WITH SPINACH
Friand de volaille en papillote

SERVES 4

4	breasts of chicken, skinned and boned
¾ pound	spinach leaves, thick stems removed
1	medium carrot
1	small leek } cut into fine julienne strips
⅛ pound	celeriac
	Salt and freshly ground pepper
½ cup	brown poultry stock (see page 21)
2 teaspoons	sherry vinegar

○ Remove the fillets from the underside of the chicken breasts.

○ Put the chicken breasts and fillets between plastic wrap and flatten them with a rolling pin.

○ Blanch the spinach in boiling salted water, then drain, and immediately dip in ice water. Drain well, then squeeze out excess moisture with a kitchen towel.

○ Sauté the vegetable julienne in a nonstick pan over gentle heat for about 5 minutes, stirring all the time.

○ Cut four large squares of aluminum foil. Place a chicken breast on each, top with the spinach, then the sautéed vegetables, then the fillet of chicken.

○ Season well with salt and pepper. Sprinkle with the stock and vinegar.

○ Seal the edges of the foil carefully, then bake in the oven at 350° F for 8 to 10 minutes.

○ Remove from the oven and serve at once. Open at the table for the full aroma to be appreciated.

CHICKEN FRICASSEE WITH VINEGAR AND TOMATO

Fricassée de volaille au vinaigre et tomate

SERVES 4

1	chicken, about 4¾ pounds
	Salt and freshly ground pepper
3	cloves of garlic, peeled and crushed
½ teaspoon	peppercorns, crushed
1	large tomato, peeled, seeded, and diced
½ cup	red wine vinegar
⅞ cup	brown poultry stock (see page 21)

○ Divide the chicken into eight pieces and carefully remove the skin. Cut off the outside part of the wings and remove any fat. Season with salt and pepper.

○ In a nonstick frying pan sauté the chicken pieces for about 4 minutes on each side.

○ Add the garlic, crushed peppercorns, and tomato and sauté for 1 minute.

○ Add the vinegar and bubble for 1 to 2 minutes to allow it to evaporate.

○ Add the poultry stock, cover, and simmer for about 2 to 3 minutes until the chicken is tender.

○ Remove the chicken from the pan and keep warm.

○ Bring the sauce to the boil and simmer gently to a thin sauce consistency. Season to taste.

○ Arrange the chicken pieces on plates and pour a little sauce over each. Serve immediately.

CHICKEN HOT POT
Pot-au-feu de volaille

SERVES 4

1	chicken, about 4¾ pounds
2 quarts	white poultry stock (see page 19)
3	onions, peeled, each studded with 2 cloves
1	bay leaf
2	cloves of garlic, peeled
	A few white peppercorns
	A bunch of herbs (such as thyme, rosemary, parsley stalks)
4	small carrots, peeled
4	pieces of celery, about 2 inches in length
4	pieces of leek, about 2 inches in length
4	small onions, peeled
1	small celeriac, peeled and cut into quarters
	Salt and freshly ground pepper
	Sprigs of parsley to garnish

○ Bring a large saucepan of water to the boil. Add the chicken and bring back to the boil. Drain and allow to cool slightly.

○ In a large pan, bring to the boil the poultry stock, onions, bay leaf, garlic, peppercorns, and herbs. Simmer for 20 minutes.

○ Add the chicken and poach for 20 minutes.

○ Remove the chicken from the pan. Strain the stock, remove the fat with strips of paper towel, and return to the rinsed-out pan. Remove the skin from the chicken.

○ Return the chicken to the pan. Add the vegetables. Bring to the boil and simmer for 10 minutes. Strain and keep the chicken and vegetables warm.

○ Boil the poultry stock rapidly to reduce by half. Adjust seasoning to taste.

○ Cut the chicken into eight pieces and arrange in soup plates with the vegetables. Pour over some stock and garnish with parsley sprigs. Serve at once.

CHICKEN SUPREME WITH WATERCRESS SAUCE
Suprême de volaille belle de nuit

The vegetables for this dish, and the herb garnish, can be changed according to the season.

SERVES 4

4	chicken breasts, about 5 ounces each, skinned, wing bone cleaned, all other bones removed
	Salt and freshly ground pepper
3	carrots, cut into fine julienne strips
3	stalks of celery, cut into fine julienne strips
5 ounces	slender green beans, cut in half lengthwise
4	stems of tarragon
4	sprigs of fresh tarragon to garnish

Sauce:

1¾ cups	white poultry stock (see page 19)
About 1½ cups	watercress leaves
¼ cup	fromage blanc (see page 29)
	Salt and freshly ground pepper
5 tablespoons	chicken or meat glaze (see page 25)

○ Season the chicken breasts with salt and pepper. Place in a steamer.

○ Put the vegetables and tarragon stems on top of chicken and steam for 4 to 5 minutes. Remove tarragon and keep the chicken warm.

○ For the sauce, place scant ½ cup of the poultry stock in a pan with the watercress leaves. Bring to the boil.

○ Allow to cool, then purée in a blender or food processor and pass through a sieve.

○ Boil the remaining poultry stock to reduce by half.

○ Whisk the fromage blanc and watercress purée into the reduced stock. Adjust seasoning to taste.

○ Pour the sauce onto four individual plates.

○ Warm the chicken or meat glaze and place in a small parchment piping bag. Snip off the end and pipe three concentric circles of glaze onto the sauce.

○ Draw a skewer across the sauce from the outside edge to the center at regular intervals to give an attractive effect.

○ Place the chicken breasts carefully in the center of each plate and garnish with tarragon.

CHICKEN BREASTS WITH SCALLIONS
Délice de volaille grillé aux ciboules

SERVES 4

1 cup	chopped scallions
3 tablespoons	chopped fresh ginger
2 teaspoons	chopped garlic
	Peel and juice of 1 lemon
	Salt and freshly ground pepper
4	chicken breasts, skinned and boned
1¾ cups	white poultry stock (see page 19)

○ Mix together three-quarters of the scallions with the ginger, garlic, lemon peel, salt, and pepper. Add the chicken breasts, cover, and marinate in the refrigerator for at least 12 hours, or up to 24 hours.

○ Pick out the lemon peel and blanch it in boiling water for 3 minutes. Cut into fine julienne strips.

○ Scrape the flavoring ingredients from the chicken and place them in a saucepan with the stock. Bring to the boil, cover, and simmer for 10 minutes. Strain, pressing with a spoon to extract all the liquid. Return the stock to a small pan and boil for 10 to 15 minutes until reduced to just under ½ cup.

○ Remove from the heat. Stir in the remaining scallions, the lemon peel, and lemon juice to taste. Season to taste with salt and pepper.

○ Grill the chicken breasts for about 4 to 5 minutes each side until cooked through but still moist.

○ Warm the sauce over gentle heat, adding a little extra stock if necessary. Cut the chicken into ½-inch slices, crosswise on the diagonal. Fan out on a serving plate and spoon the sauce around the meat.

MARINATED LEMON CHICKEN
Poularde pochée au citron naturelle

This is a very simple recipe, which can be served cold or hot. If cold, serve with a salad—Nettle Salad or Cottage Garden Salad would be ideal—and if hot, with a Rice Pilaf.

SERVES 4

1 chicken, about 4¾ pounds

Marinade:

2 quarts white poultry stock (see page 19)
Juice and grated peel of 1 lemon
Salt and freshly ground pepper

Sauce:

1 piece of lemon peel, finely chopped
1 clove
2 fresh mint leaves
¼ cup *each* of finely diced carrots, leeks, and celery
4 mint sprigs to garnish

○ In a large pot, bring the ingredients for the marinade to the boil, add the chicken, and simmer for 30 minutes.

○ Allow to cool and marinate for about 3 hours.

○ Remove the chicken from the stock and set aside. Skim stock and pour through a sieve.

○ Reduce stock to two-thirds of its original volume.

○ Add the lemon peel, clove, and mint leaves to the stock and reduce to about 1⅓ cups for the sauce.

○ Strain, add the vegetables, and bring back to the boil. Taste and add seasoning if necessary.

○ Divide the chicken into eight pieces, remove skin, and warm through in the sauce.

○ Place each portion of chicken on a warmed plate and serve with the well-seasoned sauce. Garnish with mint sprigs.

GRILLED BREAST OF DUCK WITH APPLES
Suprême de canard grillé aux pommes fruits

The recipe uses two whole ducks, but it may be more convenient to buy breasts. The apple served with the duck helps to counteract any residual richness and aids digestion.

SERVES 4

2	ducks, about 5 pounds each
⅞ cup	brown duck stock (see below and page 21)
1 tablespoon	green peppercorns, picked over and blanched
	Salt and freshly ground pepper
6 tablespoons	natural apple juice
1	eating apple, peeled, cored, and cut into eight crescents

○ Wipe the ducks clean and remove the legs carefully (keep for use in another dish). Remove breasts.

○ Cut out the collarbone and backbone and chop into small pieces. Use these, with the neck, to make the brown duck stock.

○ Boil the measured stock until reduced by half. Add the blanched peppercorns.

○ Trim the breasts and remove skin and bones. Season with salt and pepper and cook under a medium grill for 6 to 7 minutes, turning once.

○ Warm the apple juice in a saucepan. Add the apple pieces and simmer gently for 2 to 3 minutes until just tender.

○ Arrange the duck breasts on a plate and garnish with the apple pieces and peppercorns.

○ Spoon a little warmed reduced duck stock around each piece of meat and serve immediately.

GAME AND GAME BIRDS

Game is the term used for the meat of wild animals and birds. Deer and hare are the most common ground game, and their meat is nutritionally as good as that of other animals, tender and easily digestible.

The meat of feathered game—partridge, pheasant, wild duck, and guinea hen— is less rich in fat than that of domestic birds (the reason why it can so easily become dry if sautéed or grilled for too long). The flesh has a deeper and stronger taste than does poultry (thus good stocks can be made from the carcasses). Young birds have soft breast bones, a beak that is not too hard, and down under the feathers.

Contrary to general opinion, game should not be hung for too long, or until overripe, because it loses some of its essential flavor.

Use a little game herb mixture (see page 36) in the following recipes to cut down on the salt content.

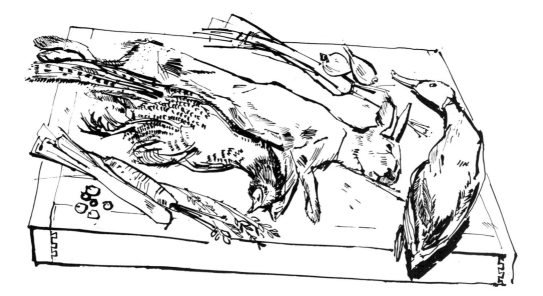

PARTRIDGE WRAPPED IN LETTUCE LEAVES
Perdreau sauté au feuilles de laitue

Handle the breasts with care, and sauté until just pink for maximum tenderness.

SERVES 4

8	large romaine lettuce leaves
8	partridge breasts, skinned and well trimmed
	Salt and freshly ground pepper
⅔ cup	game stock (see page 24)
1	small onion, peeled and finely chopped
2 ounces	mushrooms, sliced
	Cayenne
	A dash of lemon juice

○ Blanch the lettuce leaves in boiling water for 30 seconds. Dip in ice-cold water, then drain well on paper towels or a dish towel.

○ Remove the thick central rib from the leaves.

○ Season the partridge breasts with salt and pepper, then sear them quickly on both sides in a nonstick frying pan. Wrap each partridge breast in a lettuce leaf.

○ Place the lettuce packages in a gratin dish and pour the stock over them. Cover and place in a preheated oven at 400° F for 4 to 5 minutes. Strain, retaining the stock, and keep the packages warm.

○ For the sauce, sauté the onion in a nonstick pan for 1 to 2 minutes without browning. Add the mushrooms and continue to sauté for a further 1 to 2 minutes.

○ Add the stock strained from the partridge and simmer for 1 minute. Season to taste with cayenne, lemon juice, salt, and pepper.

○ Spoon a little sauce onto each of four plates. Cut the lettuce packages in diagonal slices and fan out on the sauce. Serve immediately.

BREAST OF PHEASANT
WITH ALMONDS
Délice de faisan aux amandes

The best time for eating pheasant, the most popular game bird, is from October until the end of December. Prepare while fresh or after hanging for a couple of days.

SERVES 4

2	young pheasants
	Salt and freshly ground pepper
½ cup	game stock (see page 24)
2 ounces	slivered almonds, toasted in the oven

Sauce:

2 tablespoons	finely diced shallot
3 tablespoons	finely diced celery
3 tablespoons	finely diced carrot
½	bay leaf
1	small sprig of thyme
3½ cups	game stock (see page 24)

○ Remove the breasts from the pheasants and reserve carcasses and legs for the sauce.

○ To make the sauce, chop the carcasses, legs, and necks into small pieces and place in a roasting pan.

○ Brown well in the oven at 300° F for about 40 minutes.

○ Add the sauce vegetables and herbs, stir well, and return to the oven for a further 10 minutes. Remove from the oven.

○ Add one-third of the stock and allow to simmer on top of the stove, uncovered, until it reaches a syrupy consistency. Add another third of the stock and repeat the boiling-down process.

○ Add the remainder of the stock and boil down to ⅔ cup. Strain and season to taste.

○ Trim the pheasant breasts, season with salt and pepper, and sauté in a nonstick frying pan for about 5 to 6 minutes, turning once. Remove from pan and keep warm.

○ Pour off any fat from the pan and add the ½ cup of game stock. Bring to the boil and reduce by half, then add to the sauce. Keep warm.

○ Cut the pheasant breasts carefully into thin slices.

○ Arrange on a suitable dish and sprinkle with slivered almonds. Serve the sauce separately.

WILD DUCK WITH ONION CONFIT
Canard sauvage aux oignons rouges

SERVES 4

4	breasts of wild young duck, skinned and trimmed
1	large red onion, finely sliced
3 tablespoons	red wine vinegar
1⅓ cups	wild duck stock (use carcass and legs, and see also page 24)
1 to 2 tablespoons	clear honey
	Salt and freshly ground pepper

○ Lightly grill the seasoned wild duck breasts until pink, about 4 to 5 minutes. Keep warm.

○ Meanwhile, sweat the onion in a nonstick pan until light brown, stirring constantly.

○ Add the red wine vinegar and reduce by half.

○ Add the duck stock and reduce by half.

○ Add honey to the sauce to taste and season well with salt and pepper.

○ Cut the breasts of duck lengthwise into ¼-inch slices.

○ Pour the sauce onto four warmed plates and lay the slices of duck on top. Serve immediately.

BREAST OF GUINEA HEN
WITH LEEK AND WILD MUSHROOMS
Suprême de pintade aux fruits des bois

Depending on seasonal availability, different varieties of mushrooms can
be used in this dish.

SERVES 4

4	breasts of guinea hen, about 5 ounces each, wing bones cleaned and trimmed
	Salt and freshly ground pepper
2½ tablespoons	finely chopped shallots
7 ounces	oyster mushrooms } cleaned, washed, and
5 ounces	chanterelles } cut in half
3 or 4	medium leeks cut in 2-inch lengths and blanched for 30 seconds
	A few sprigs of chervil to garnish

○ Season the guinea hen breasts with salt and pepper.

○ Sauté them in a nonstick frying pan for about 3 minutes, turning once. Remove from the pan and keep warm.

○ Add the finely chopped shallots to the pan and sauté, stirring constantly, until transparent. Remove from the pan and reserve.

○ Add the oyster mushrooms and chanterelles to the hot pan and sauté for about 1 minute.

○ Add the well-drained leeks and stir constantly for a further minute.

○ Return the shallots to the pan and season with salt and pepper.

○ Place the guinea hen breasts on the vegetables in the pan, cover with foil, and heat gently for another minute.

○ Arrange on four individual plates and garnish with sprigs of chervil.

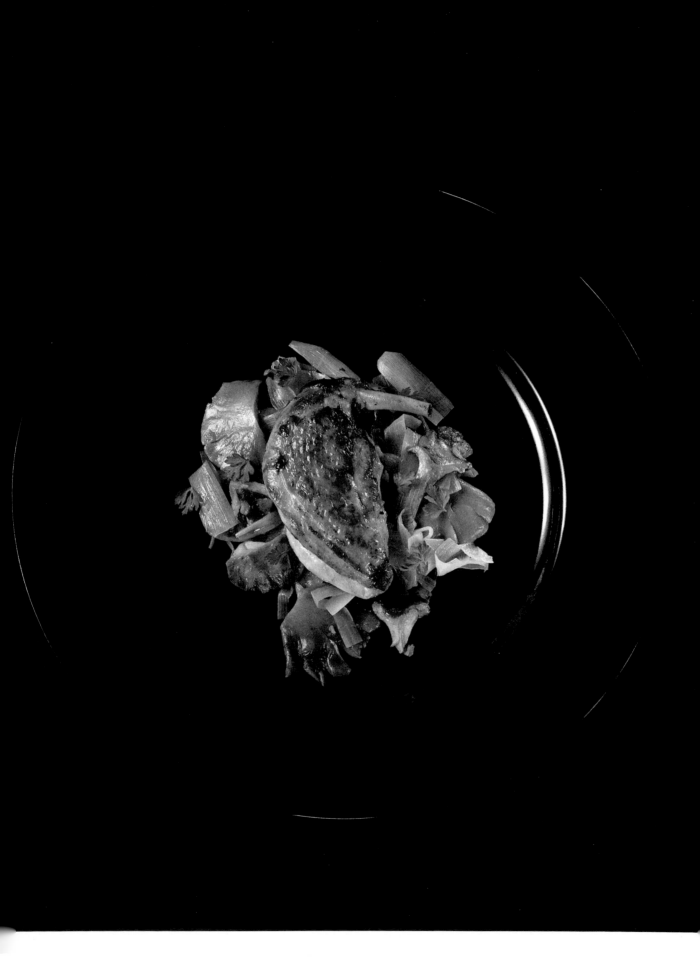

WARM GUINEA HEN
WITH CABBAGE SALAD
Pintade tiède à la salade de choux

SERVES 4

2	guinea hens, about 2 pounds each
3 cups	shredded white cabbage
3 cups	shredded savoy cabbage
3 tablespoons	red wine vinegar
1½ ounces	prosciutto, cut into julienne strips
	Salt and freshly ground pepper
	A selection of washed and dried salad leaves, such as lamb's lettuce, endive, chicory, radicchio, and julienne of carrot (blanched)

○ Bone the guinea hens and remove the skin. Reserve the breasts and slice the leg meat.

○ Sauté the sliced meat in a nonstick pan for about 2 minutes. Remove and keep warm.

○ Sauté the breasts in the nonstick pan for about 4 to 5 minutes, turning once, until golden. Remove from the pan and keep warm.

○ Add the cabbage to the pan and sauté for 2 to 3 minutes, stirring constantly. Add the vinegar.

○ Combine the prosciutto and sliced meat with the cabbage and season with salt and pepper to taste.

○ Place the salad leaves on four individual plates and arrange the cabbage salad on top.

○ Cut the guinea hen breasts into thin slices and arrange in a fan on the top of each salad. Serve immediately.

MEDALLIONS OF HARE WITH GRAPES
Médaillons de lièvre aux raisins

Prime-quality hares are about 4 to 8 months old, with a paler meat than
older animals.

SERVES 4

20	medallions of young hare (cut from the saddle), about 1 ounce each, well trimmed and any sinews removed
	Salt and freshly ground pepper
¼ cup	finely chopped shallots
6	juniper berries, roughly crushed
1 tablespoon	thyme leaves
6	peppercorns, roughly crushed
1¾ cups	game stock (see page 24)
20	large white grapes, skinned, and seeds removed with a skewer
2 teaspoons	lemon juice
5 ounces	chanterelles, cleaned and washed

○ Season the medallions of hare with salt and pepper.

○ Sauté them in a nonstick pan for about 2 minutes on each side until pink. Remove from the pan and keep warm.

○ Add the shallots to the pan and sauté, stirring constantly, until transparent.

○ Add the juniper berries, thyme leaves, and peppercorns. Mix well and sauté for 1 minute.

○ Add the game stock and boil rapidly to reduce by half.

○ Strain the sauce and season to taste.

○ Place the grapes in a minimum of water flavored with the lemon juice and heat gently for 1 minute.

○ Sauté the prepared chanterelles in a nonstick pan for 1 minute, stirring all the time. Season to taste.

○ Arrange five medallions of hare on each of four individual plates. Spoon the sauce over the meat.

○ Arrange the chanterelles in the center of the meat and garnish with the well-drained grapes.

GRILLED MEDALLIONS OF VENISON WITH CRANBERRIES
Mignons de chevreuil grillés aux airelles

Venison is a very lean meat. It is relatively low in calories and high in iron and some vitamins. Animals under about 2 years have tender and easily digestible meat, but older animals are tougher.

SERVES 4

12	medallions of venison, about 1½ ounces each, well trimmed
	Salt and freshly ground pepper
¼ cup	orange juice
	Juice of ½ lemon
2 teaspoons	honey
About ½ pound	cranberries, washed
2 tablespoons	finely chopped shallots
11 ounces	small chanterelles, cleaned, washed, and dried
1 teaspoon	finely chopped thyme
½ teaspoon	finely cut sage
1⅓ cups	game stock (see page 24), reduced by half

○ Season the medallions on both sides.

○ Grill them at a high temperature for 1 minute on each side and keep warm.

○ Bring the orange and lemon juices and honey to the boil.

○ Add the cranberries and simmer for 30 seconds.

○ Sauté the shallots in a nonstick pan until transparent, stirring constantly.

○ Add the well-dried chanterelles and sauté for about 2 minutes. Season with salt and pepper to taste.

○ Add the thyme and sage to the reduced stock and arrange this sauce on four individual plates.

○ Place the medallions, three each, on the sauce and put 1 teaspoon of cranberries on each medallion.

○ Garnish with the chanterelles and serve immediately.

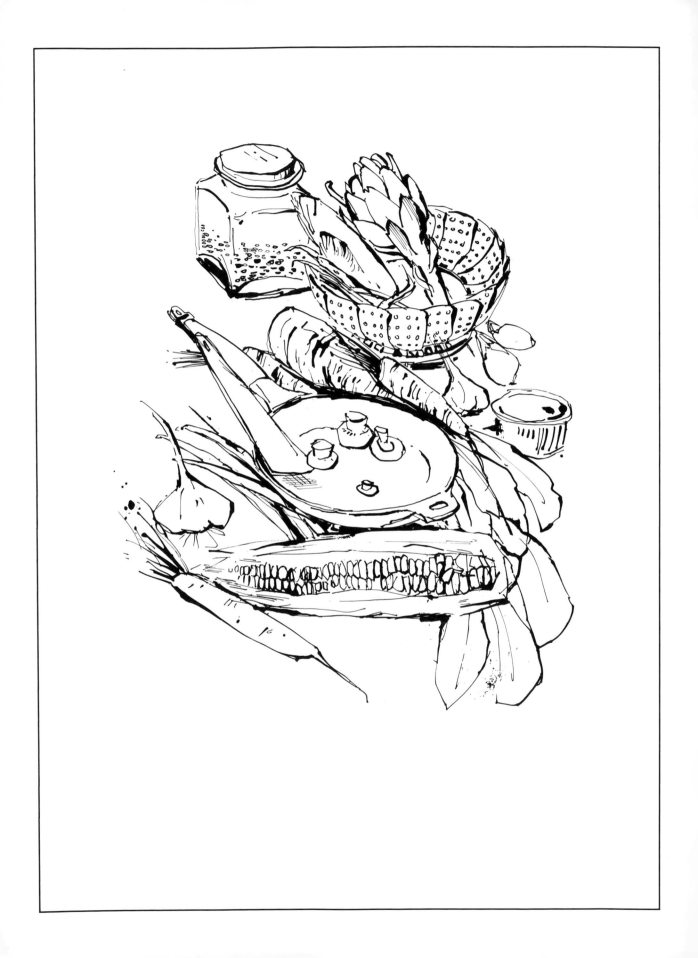

VEGETABLES

Vegetables should—and do—play a very large part in the preparation and presentation of a wide range of dishes. Many vegetables are colorful and of wonderful shapes, and they add immeasurably to the finished look of a dish. Their flavors, too, are natural and subtle, complementing many other foods.

But the principal value of vegetables lies in their nutritional content. They are a major source of cellulose or fiber, which is recognized as vital for health; and they also contain many vitamins and minerals not freely available from other foods.

To retain their benefits, however, vegetables need careful handling. Obviously, the fresher the better; vitamins A, C, B_1, and B_2 decrease daily after a vegetable is taken from the ground or plucked from the plant. They should never be stored for long. Cleaning, washing, and preparation are other danger areas. Vitamin C is water soluble, so may leach out if the vegetable is soaked; vitamins B_1 and B_2 and some minerals (calcium, for example) may also be thus lost. Vegetables should also be cut or chopped just before use because many lose their nutrients through contact with air as well as water—it is the vitamin C oxidizing that turns potatoes brown (as well as fruits like apples) after being cut. This also affects flavor.

All previous efforts are wasted, however, if mistakes are made during cooking. Most vitamins and minerals will be lost if the vegetable is boiled for too long. (For this reason, it is always advisable to use vegetable water and its nutrients—in stocks, for instance.) Savoy cabbage boiled until it has lost its color would lose 65 percent of its vitamin C content and cauliflower 90 percent (the latter is a good source of phosphorus, which would also be lost). If, however, the vegetables were steamed, approximately 80 percent of their vitamin C would be retained. Vegetables, to sum up, should be handled with the utmost care to protect their nutrients, color, flavor, and shape. Barely cook them so that they still remain crisp and delicious, unless using them for a purée.

Rice, millet, and lentils are also used as vegetable accompaniments, and they are high in food value, containing protein and fiber. Many of the healthiest cuisines in the world have a basis in legumes and grains such as these. Brown rice is rice in its natural state after the husks have been removed; it has a stronger taste and is easier to digest than white rice but takes longer to cook. Millet, another cereal plant, comes in many varieties and is a major world food crop. Lentils are among the most popular legumes.

Use an herb mixture (see page 36) in place of some seasoning to cut down on salt content.

Note:
The servings in this chapter are intended as garnishes to accompany meat, poultry, game, or fish dishes. They may be served in combination, or quantities may be increased, if you wish.

VEGETABLE GOULASH
WITH ROSEMARY AND MARJORAM
Goulasch de légumes aux herbes

Other squash or pumpkin, green or yellow peppers—whatever is colorful and available—can be used in this flexible recipe.

SERVES 4

½	medium onion, sliced
4	large tomatoes, peeled and chopped
2	zucchini, sliced
2	large red peppers, cored and diced
1	clove of garlic, peeled and crushed
½ teaspoon	tiny rosemary sprigs
½ teaspoon	marjoram leaves
	Salt and freshly ground pepper

○ Sauté the onion carefully in a nonstick pan, stirring constantly, until transparent but not browned.

○ Add the tomatoes, zucchini, and red pepper.

○ Stir in the garlic and herbs.

○ Cover and simmer for 3 to 4 minutes until just tender.

○ Season to taste with salt and pepper and serve immediately.

ZUCCHINI WITH LETTUCE AND SORREL SAUCE

Courgettes, sauce à la laitue et à l'oseille

SERVES 4

½	small onion, finely chopped
½	head of lettuce, cut into strips
2 tablespoons	fresh sorrel, cut into strips
⅞ cup	white poultry stock (see page 19)
½ cup	cottage cheese, strained
1	egg yolk
	Salt and freshly ground pepper
1 pound	zucchini, thinly sliced

○ Sauté the onion, lettuce, and sorrel, stirring gently for 2 to 3 minutes, in a non-stick pan.

○ Add the stock and simmer, covered, for 5 to 6 minutes. Blend in a food processor or blender.

○ Return to the pan and stir in the cottage cheese mixed with the egg yolk; heat gently, stirring, until thickened. Do not let the sauce boil. Season to taste with salt and pepper.

○ Steam the zucchini for 2 to 3 minutes. Season with salt and pepper.

○ Pour the sauce onto a plate and arrange the zucchini slices on top.

STUFFED TOMATOES WITH SPINACH
Tomates farcies aux épinards

Serve these tomatoes on their own as a vegetable accompaniment, or as
a first course, arranged in soup plates with yellow pepper sauce.

SERVES 4

4	medium, ripe tomatoes
	Salt
2½ tablespoons	finely chopped shallots
About ½ pound	leaf spinach, stems removed, blanched and roughly chopped
¼ cup	cottage cheese
	Nutmeg and freshly ground pepper
4	sprigs of chervil

Yellow pepper sauce (optional, see above):

2	medium yellow peppers, washed and trimmed
1 tablespoon	finely chopped shallots
1	small clove of garlic, peeled and chopped
	A few sprigs of fresh thyme
1¾ cups	vegetable stock (see page 26)
	A pinch of sugar
	Salt and freshly ground pepper

○ Cut open the stem end of each tomato with a knife, take out the middle with a teaspoon, and season the tomatoes with salt.

○ Sauté the shallots in a nonstick pan, stirring carefully, until they are soft and transparent but not colored.

○ Add the well-drained spinach and sauté for about 2 minutes.

○ Add the cottage cheese and season with salt, nutmeg, and pepper.

○ Carefully fill the tomatoes with the spinach mixture.

○ Place in an ovenproof nonstick pan, cover with foil, and heat in a moderate oven (350° F) for about 4 to 5 minutes.

○ If you wish to serve the tomatoes with the yellow pepper sauce, cut the peppers into large pieces. Sweat the shallots and garlic in a nonstick pan over gentle heat without browning. Add the yellow peppers, thyme, and vegetable stock and simmer, uncovered, for about 20 minutes until pepper is tender. Purée in a food processor or blender and season to taste with sugar, salt, and pepper.

○ Serve as desired (see above), garnished with a sprig of chervil.

LEAF SPINACH
WITH COTTAGE CHEESE
Épinards en feuilles Palace

SERVES 4

1 pound	young spinach, without stems
1½ tablespoons	finely chopped shallot
1	clove of garlic, unpeeled
¼ cup	cottage cheese
	Salt, freshly ground pepper, and nutmeg

○ Wash the spinach leaves well, then dry.

○ Sweat the finely chopped shallot and the whole garlic clove carefully in a nonstick pan without coloring them.

○ Add the spinach leaves and sweat well for 3 to 4 minutes.

○ Add the cottage cheese and stir through.

○ Season with salt, freshly ground pepper, and nutmeg.

○ Remove the clove of garlic before serving.

SAUTEED PARSNIPS WITH SESAME SEEDS
Panais sautés aux sésames

The sweetness of the parsnips forms a delicious combination with the nutty flavor of the sautéed sesame seeds—which are high in protein and a good source of B vitamins and minerals.

SERVES 4

1 tablespoon	sesame seeds
1 pound	parsnips, peeled, quartered lengthwise, and thinly sliced
4	scallions, cut in 1-inch pieces
1	clove of garlic, peeled and chopped
¼ pound	snowpeas, trimmed and cut in half lengthwise
	Salt and freshly ground pepper

○ Sauté the seeds carefully until golden brown in a nonstick pan.

○ Add the parsnips, scallion pieces, and garlic and sauté for 5 minutes until just tender.

○ Add the snowpeas and sauté for another minute.

○ Season to taste with salt and pepper and serve immediately.

ENDIVES AND MUSHROOMS GLAZED WITH CHEESE

Endives Belges et champignons gratinés

SERVES 4

4	large endives
5 ounces	small button mushrooms
½ cup	white poultry or vegetable stock (see pages 19 or 26)
2 teaspoons	lemon juice
1 teaspoon	honey
	Salt and freshly ground pepper
2 ounces	Gouda cheese, grated

○ Wash the endives well, cut off ½ inch at the bottom, and then break into separate leaves. Place in a saucepan.

○ Place the mushrooms in another pan.

○ Divide the stock and lemon juice between the two pans. Add the honey to the endives.

○ Cook the endives quickly for 1 to 2 minutes until just tender. Drain and arrange in a small gratin dish.

○ Bring the endive stock to the boil and boil rapidly to reduce to 1 tablespoon. Spoon over the endives.

○ Sauté the mushrooms quickly until no liquid remains.

○ Spoon mushrooms over the endives and season with salt and pepper to taste.

○ Sprinkle with grated cheese and bubble under a hot grill until golden.

GLAZED SHALLOTS
Échalotes glacées

Scallions or pearl onions may be prepared in the same way as the shallots.

SERVES 4

½ pound	small shallots
½ cup	apple juice
1 cup	water
	Salt and freshly ground pepper

○ Carefully remove the root part of the shallots, then peel them, leaving them whole.

○ Heat a nonstick pan, add the shallots, and sweat over low heat.

○ Add the apple juice and allow to caramelize by tipping the pan; do not stir.

○ Add the water and salt and pepper to taste.

○ Cover and simmer over low heat for 10 to 12 minutes.

○ Remove the shallots and reduce the liquid to about 2 tablespoons.

○ Replace the shallots in the sauce and serve immediately.

CARROT AND SPINACH MOUSSE
Mousseline de carottes et épinards

These mousseline shapes look and taste wonderful and go well with any meat dish.

SERVES 4

For carrot layer:

½ pound	carrots, thinly sliced
4 tablespoons	tofu
	Salt and freshly ground pepper
1	egg white

For spinach layer:

½ pound	spinach leaves, washed and thick stems removed
6 to 7 tablespoons	tofu
	Freshly grated nutmeg
	Salt and freshly ground pepper
1	egg white

○ Cook the carrots in a minimum of boiling salted water until tender, about 3 to 4 minutes. Drain.

○ Add the tofu to the drained carrots and make into a purée. Season to taste with salt and pepper.

○ Whisk the egg white to a soft peak and fold into the purée.

○ Cook the spinach over gentle heat without extra water until tender and dry.

○ Mix with the tofu and make into a purée. Season with nutmeg, salt, and pepper.

○ Whisk egg white to a soft peak and fold into the purée.

○ Divide the carrot purée among four individual ramekins and level the surface. Top with the spinach purée and level the surface.

○ Cover with foil and cook in a bain-marie in the oven at 350° F for 25 to 30 minutes until just firm to the touch. (A toothpick will come out of the mousse clean when it is cooked.)

○ Cool slightly, then invert onto a serving dish.

ARTICHOKE MOUSSE
Purée d'artichauts

This mousse goes well with meat dishes, particularly lamb.

SERVES 4

3	large globe artichokes
3 tablespoons	cottage cheese
1	egg
1 teaspoon	finely cut chervil leaves
	Dash of lemon juice
	Salt and freshly ground pepper

Sauce:

2 tablespoons	cottage cheese
½ cup	low-fat natural yogurt (see page 31)
2 teaspoons	finely cut chervil leaves
	Pinch of cayenne
	Salt
	Parsley sprigs to garnish

○ Break off the stems of the artichokes so that the tough fibers come away from the bottoms.

○ Cook the artichokes in lightly salted water for 30 to 40 minutes (they are cooked when the leaves can be pulled away easily).

○ When cool, take off the leaves, remove and discard the hairy choke, and chop the artichoke bottoms. Using a spoon, scrape the flesh from the base of each leaf.

○ Purée all the artichoke flesh with the cottage cheese and egg. Stir in the chervil and season to taste with lemon juice, salt, and pepper.

○ Spoon the mixture into four individual nonstick molds. Cover with foil and cook in a bain-marie in the oven at 325° F for 20 to 25 minutes until just firm to the touch. Allow to cool slightly.

○ Mix together all the ingredients for the sauce, bring to the boil, and season well.

○ Set the mousses in the center of each of four plates. Spoon a little sauce around each one and garnish with parsley sprigs.

FRESH CORN GALETTE
Galette de maïs

These small pancakes make a very good accompaniment to grilled meat
and poultry. Corn contains fiber and vitamin C.

SERVES 4

3 or 4	ears of corn
⅔ cup	skim milk
½ cup	fromage blanc (see page 29)
1	egg
1	egg yolk
	Generous ½ cup flour
	Salt, a little freshly ground nutmeg, and pepper

○ Wash the corn well and blanch in the milk.

○ Remove the corn from the cob and chop the kernels roughly. Keep the milk for
the batter.

○ Mix together the milk, fromage blanc, egg, egg yolk, and flour. Do it fairly slowly
to avoid lumps.

○ Add the roughly chopped corn and flavor with salt, nutmeg, and pepper.

○ Heat a nonstick frying pan, measure out small pancakes with a tablespoon, and
sauté until golden brown on both sides.

RICE PILAF
Riz pilaf

Rice is the largest food crop in the world. Brown rice still has the bran coating, which is removed from white rice, and thus retains all the valuable proteins and minerals as well as fiber.

SERVES 4

2½ tablespoons	finely chopped onion
1 cup	brown long-grain rice
1⅓ cups	vegetable stock (see page 26)
	Salt and freshly ground pepper

○ Sauté the onion carefully in a nonstick pan until transparent, stirring constantly.

○ Transfer to a suitable flame- and ovenproof casserole. Add the rice, vegetable stock, and salt and pepper to taste.

○ Bring to the boil on top of the stove, then cover with a piece of parchment or wax paper and a lid, and place in the oven at 350° F. Leave for about 20 to 25 minutes, stirring occasionally.

○ Remove from the casserole and taste for seasoning. Fluff up with a fork and serve immediately.

VEGETABLE RICE
WITH TOASTED HAZELNUTS
Riz et légumes aux noisettes

Hazelnuts, most commonly used in cakes and sweet dishes, here lend their flavor and goodness to a savory rice accompaniment. They are lower in calories than most other nuts.

SERVES 4

1 cup	hazelnuts
1	medium onion, peeled and chopped
1	clove of garlic, crushed
1⅛ cups	brown long-grain rice
2 cups	water
½ teaspoon	turmeric
1	large carrot, scraped and diced
½ pound	slender green beans, cut into 2-inch pieces
1	small red pepper, seeded and finely cut
4	tomatoes, peeled and quartered
	Salt and freshly ground pepper

○ Toast the nuts in the oven at 350° F for about 10 minutes.

○ Sauté the onion and garlic in a nonstick pan, stirring constantly, until they are soft and transparent but not colored.

○ Add the rice, water, turmeric, and a little salt and bring to the boil. Cover and simmer very gently for about 30 minutes until the rice is tender.

○ Meanwhile, cook the carrot, beans, and pepper in boiling salted water until tender, about 3 to 5 minutes. Drain.

○ Using a fork, carefully mix the cooked vegetables and tomatoes into the rice, together with half the toasted hazelnuts. Season to taste with salt and pepper.

○ Serve in a large shallow dish, sprinkled with the remaining hazelnuts.

BRAISED LENTILS
Lentilles braisées

SERVES 4

1	medium onion ⎫
1	carrot ⎬ finely cut
1	small leek ⎭
⅔ cup	diced potatoes
3 tablespoons	tomato concassé (see page 33)
2½ cups	brown veal stock (see page 22)
1	small clove of garlic, pressed
1 cup	lentils, soaked for 1 hour and drained well
	Salt and freshly ground pepper
2 teaspoons	wine vinegar

○ Sauté the vegetables and tomato concassé in a nonstick pan, stirring all the time, for about 3 to 4 minutes. Add the veal stock and garlic.

○ Add the well-drained lentils and bring to the boil.

○ Season with salt and pepper. Skim and simmer until just tender, about 30 minutes.

○ Remove the garlic.

○ Purée a quarter of the cooked lentils in a food processor or blender and stir the rest of the lentils into the purée.

○ Finally, add the vinegar and season with salt and pepper.

MILLET PILAF
Pilaf de millet

Millet is very mild in flavor, but combined with the ingredients below,
it provides a tasty accompaniment for meat, especially beef.

SERVES 4

9 ounces	millet
1 quart	vegetable stock (see page 26)
1 tablespoon	brewer's yeast
1 tablespoon	soy sauce
½ cup	cottage cheese
	Salt and freshly ground pepper

○ Place the millet in a nonstick pan over medium heat and sauté until golden colored, stirring occasionally, about 5 to 8 minutes.

○ Add the stock and simmer gently for 30 to 40 minutes until all the stock is absorbed and the millet is tender.

○ Add the yeast, stir in the soy sauce and cottage cheese, and serve at once. Adjust seasoning to taste.

YOUNG NETTLE AND POTATO PUREE
Purée d'orties et pommes de terre

Wherever man settles in the Northern Hemisphere, nettles appear. They are "culture followers" and indicate nitrogenous ground. They are also full of goodness—containing several vitamins, tannin, mineral salts, and iron—but only the youngest nettle tops must be used. Spinach leaves can replace some of the nettles in this recipe if desired.

SERVES 4

½ pound	young nettle tops
1	small potato, peeled and diced
About 2 cups	vegetable stock (see page 26)
	Freshly grated nutmeg
	Salt and freshly ground pepper
½ cup	fromage blanc (see page 29)

○ Pick the nettle tops carefully, preferably with gloves. Wash them well in salted water, then drain.

○ Place the nettles, potato, and stock in a saucepan. Cover and simmer for 20 minutes, adding more stock if necessary.

○ Pour off any excess liquid and purée the mixture in a food processor or blender.

○ Season the purée well with nutmeg, salt, and pepper, then stir in the fromage blanc.

POTATOES WITH GOAT CHEESE
Pommes de terre au fromage de chèvre

By the time the potatoes are soft, the liquid has been absorbed, making a wonderful soft, tasty accompaniment to many grilled meat dishes. Goat cheese gives it a different and special flavor, but other cheeses may be used to reduce fat and calorie content.

SERVES 4

1 pound	medium potatoes, peeled and washed
	Salt and freshly ground pepper
1	small clove of garlic, peeled and cut in half
About 1 cup	vegetable stock (see page 26)
3 to 4 ounces	soft goat cheese, crushed into small pieces

○ Cut the potatoes into ⅛-inch-thick slices, then place on a cloth to dry. Season with salt and pepper.

○ Rub a suitable gratin dish with the cut clove of garlic.

○ Arrange the potato slices in the dish in layers.

○ Add the vegetable stock and bake in a preheated oven at 375° F for about 30 minutes.

○ About 5 minutes before the end of cooking time, sprinkle the cheese over the potatoes, return to the oven, and bake for a few minutes longer until golden brown.

POTATOES SAUTEED WITH HAM
Pommes de terre sautées au jambon

Prosciutto or smoked ham can be used instead of cooked ham. All fat
must be removed from ham, whatever kind, before use. Serve with any
meat dish.

SERVES 4

1 pound	medium potatoes, washed, peeled, and grated
½	medium onion, sliced
2 ounces	cooked ham, without fat, cut into fine julienne strips
	Salt and freshly ground pepper

○ Dry the potatoes thoroughly on a cloth.

○ Sauté the onion in a nonstick pan until transparent, stirring constantly.

○ Add the ham and sauté for 2 minutes.

○ Add the well-dried potatoes and season with salt and pepper. Sauté until light brown in color.

○ Form the contents of the pan into a cake shape, using a metal spatula (or wooden spoon). Press heavily so that the potato strips stick together.

○ Sauté the ham and potato "cake" on both sides until golden brown.

JACQUELINE POTATOES
Pommes de terre Jacqueline

These attractive potato shapes are an ideal accompaniment for any meat dish, especially Fillet of Beef with Rosemary and Mustard.

SERVES 4

1 pound   medium potatoes, peeled and washed
¼ cup   fromage blanc (see page 29)
        Salt, freshly ground pepper, and nutmeg

○ Cut the potatoes into ⅛-inch slices, using a knife, mandoline, or food processor, then pat dry with a cloth.

○ Place in a bowl, add the fromage blanc, and season with salt, pepper, and nutmeg. Mix well.

○ Using any small mold (little aluminum containers work well), one or more per person, depending on size, fill them with overlapping circles of potato slices coated with fromage blanc.

○ Bake in the oven at 375° F for about 12 minutes.

○ Ease the potatoes out of the molds with a metal spatula or small knife and serve immediately.

DESSERTS

Desserts are synonymous in many people's minds with some of the excluded ingredients of Cuisine Naturelle—butter, cream, and sugar, and thus pastry, chocolate, and many other basics of the art of dessert preparation. But by omitting butter and cream and using yogurt or quark instead, and by cutting down on traditional quantities of sugar, relying more on the natural sugars in fruit, for instance, the following desserts represent a good variety of healthy and delicious finales to any meal. And because they *are* the finale, the last memory of a wonderful meal, they must also *look* spectacular.

The majority of the recipes use fresh fruit in some form or another, served raw to conserve their abundant vitamin C, or prepared simply in any way. There are ice creams (made with yogurt), sherbets, terrines, and mousses. Soft fruits are made—with brown bread—into a magnificent summer pudding or piled into the very lightest filo pastry strudel or a thin lacework tuile basket. And to complete the selection there is a trio of healthful petits fours.

YOGURT FRUIT ICE
Glace de yogourt et fruits

In this and the following yogurt ices, the cream or milk is replaced by
yogurt, which is much lower in calories.

SERVES 4

1 pint	berries (strawberries, raspberries, or other fruits)
2 tablespoons	lemon juice
⅓ cup	low-fat natural yogurt (see page 31)
⅓ cup	superfine sugar
⅓ cup	quark (see page 30)

○ Purée the fruits with the lemon juice in a food processor or blender.

○ Whisk together the yogurt and sugar and mix with the fruit purée.

○ Beat the quark until smooth and carefully fold into the mixture.

○ Freeze immediately, whisking the ice vigorously from time to time, or transfer to
an electric ice cream maker and freeze.

GOAT'S MILK YOGURT RASPBERRY ICE
Glace de yogourt de chèvre et framboise

Similar goat's milk yogurt ices could be made with red currants and blueberries, and they all could, naturally, be made with ordinary low-fat natural yogurt.

SERVES 4

About 1 pint	raspberries
4 tablespoons	superfine sugar
1¼ cups	goat's milk yogurt (see page 31)
2	egg yolks
3 tablespoons	water

○ Push the raspberries through a sieve and mix with half the sugar and the yogurt.

○ Beat the egg yolks until creamy.

○ Boil the remaining sugar and water together at 245° F until the bubbles settle and flatten.

○ Using an electric beater turned on full, gradually pour the hot syrup into the egg yolks and keep beating until the mixture is cold and thick.

○ Stir the yogurt mixture carefully into the egg yolk cream and put into a 2½-cup mold, and freeze for 2 to 3 hours, whisking the ice vigorously from time to time. Before dividing into portions allow to thaw in the refrigerator for 20 minutes.

OATMEAL ICE CREAM
Glace d'avoine

SERVES 4

⅓ cup	oatmeal
4 tablespoons	superfine sugar
2	egg yolks
⅔ cup	skim milk
1⅓ cups	low-fat natural yogurt (see page 31)
½ pint	raspberries, to decorate

○ Place the oatmeal in a nonstick pan and sauté over gentle heat until golden brown. Remove from the pan and let cool.

○ Whisk together the sugar and egg yolks.

○ Heat the milk to body temperature and stir into the egg mixture.

○ Place in a double boiler or in a bowl over simmering water and cook until the mixture is thick enough to coat the back of a wooden spoon. Cool.

○ Stir in the oatmeal and yogurt.

○ Freeze immediately, whisking the ice vigorously from time to time.

○ Serve ice cream in scoops, decorated with raspberries.

MELON SHERBET
Sorbet de melon

SERVES 4

1⅛ cups   water
4 tablespoons   sugar
1   ripe melon, about 1¾ to 2 pounds
   Juice of 1 lime

○ Bring the water and sugar to the boil. Allow to cool.

○ Divide the melon into eight, remove the seeds and skin, cut the flesh into cubes, and purée with the lime juice in a food processor or blender.

○ Mix the fruit purée with the cold sugar and water mixture.

○ Freeze immediately, whisking the ice vigorously from time to time, or put in an electric ice cream maker.

APPLE SHERBET
Sorbet de pommes fruits

SERVES 4

About 1 pound   eating apples
⅞ cup   unfiltered apple juice
   Juice of 1 lime

○ Peel the apples, cut into quarters, and remove the cores, then slice.

○ Bring the apple and lime juices to the boil and cook the apples in the liquid until soft.

○ Purée the apples and liquid in a food processor or blender and freeze, whisking the ice crystals vigorously from time to time, or put in an electric ice cream maker.

SPICED SHERBET
Sorbet d'épices

This sherbet may be served after fish or between a fish and main dish, providing the meal has more than four courses. To vary the recipe, add a split vanilla bean or 2 cinnamon sticks instead of the saffron to the water and sugar, bring to the boil, and cook for 1 minute. Let cool. Remove the vanilla bean or cinnamon sticks and continue as below.

SERVES 4

1¾ cups	water
6 tablespoons	sugar
	A large pinch of saffron strands
3 tablespoons	lime juice
1	egg white

○ Bring the water, 3½ tablespoons sugar, and the saffron to the boil and cook for 1 minute, stirring constantly. Allow to cool.

○ Strain the lime juice and mix with the sugar syrup.

○ Whisk the egg white until stiff, then whisk in the remaining sugar.

○ Carefully fold the whipped egg white into the completely cooled liquid and then freeze, whisking the ice vigorously from time to time, or transfer to an electric ice cream maker and freeze.

BLACK SPOOM

A spoom is a sherbet with added egg whites, and black spoom is a sherbet made with black tea. The tea should be infused; do not boil, or the fine flavor is lost and it becomes bitter.

Try your own mixtures of teas. You can use Earl Grey, Darjeeling, Lapsang Souchong, or green China tea. You could also try herb, fruit, or flower teas, such as hawthorn blossom, elderflower, woodruff blossom, rosehip, fresh mint, or fresh lemon mint.

SERVES 4

1¾ cups	sparkling mineral water
2 tablespoons	black tea (flowery orange Pekoe quality)
5 tablespoons	sugar
1 to 2	egg whites

○ Bring the mineral water to the boil.

○ Put the tea leaves into a jug and pour on the boiling water.

○ Let the tea infuse for 2 minutes.

○ Stir, strain the tea, and add the sugar. Continue to stir until the sugar dissolves. Cool.

○ Beat the egg whites until stiff.

○ Carefully fold the egg whites into the completely cold liquid and freeze. Whisk the ice vigorously from time to time, or transfer to an electric ice cream maker and freeze.

COFFEE ICE
Mocca Granité

Granité, gremolata, or granita is nearest to the original sherbet—hardly sweetened and with fairly large ice crystals. The thickness of the sherbet and size of the ice crystals depend on the amount of sugar or sweetening used and on how much it is stirred during freezing.

SERVES 4

2 tablespoons	coffee beans, dark roasted
1¾ cups	water, brought to the boil
2 tablespoons	clear honey

○ Coarsely grind the coffee beans or crush them in a mortar.

○ Put the coffee in a pan and pour on the boiling water.

○ Cover and put the pan in a warm bain-marie for 15 minutes to allow the coffee to brew.

○ Strain the coffee and immediately add the honey. Stir until the honey is well blended.

○ Allow the coffee syrup to cool.

○ Pour the cooled coffee syrup into a container and place in the freezer for 2 to 3 hours.

○ Stir every 30 minutes with a spoon.

○ Serve scooped into individual glasses.

SYMPHONY OF FRUIT MOUSSES
Symphonie de mousses aux fruits

SERVES 8

Raspberry mousse:

2	eggs, separated
2 tablespoons	superfine sugar
1⅓ tablespoons	gelatin
Scant 1 pint	raspberries, puréed and strained
¼ cup	quark (see page 30)

Mango mousse:

2	eggs, separated
2 tablespoons	superfine sugar
1⅓ tablespoons	gelatin
1	large mango, about ¾ pound, peeled, puréed, and strained
1 teaspoon	lemon juice
¼ cup	quark (see page 30)

Lime mousse:

2	eggs, separated
2 tablespoons	superfine sugar
1⅓ tablespoons	gelatin
	Zest and strained juice of 3 limes
¼ cup	quark (see page 30)

Mango sauce:

1	mango, about 1 to 1¼ pounds, peeled and puréed
	Lemon juice to taste

Raspberry sauce:

Generous pint	raspberries
4 teaspoons	confectioner's sugar
	Lemon juice to taste

Garnish:

  8   raspberries, nice and ripe
24   mint leaves

The three mousses are made in the same way:

○ Whisk the egg yolks with the sugar in a bowl over hot water until pale and thick.

○ Soften the gelatin in 2 tablespoons water and heat gently until dissolved.

○ Stir the gelatin into the fruit purée and add lemon or lime juice if specified.

○ Whisk in the egg mixture and cool.

○ Whisk in the quark and chill until just beginning to set.

○ Whisk the egg whites until stiff.

○ Fold into the fruit mixture and chill until set.

○ To make the mango sauce, mix together the mango purée and a little water and simmer gently for 2 to 3 minutes. Cool and stir in a little lemon juice to taste. Strain.

○ To make the raspberry sauce, purée and strain the raspberries. Stir in the confectioner's sugar and lemon juice to taste. Reduce half the raspberry sauce by one-third to get a darker color.

○ To serve, shape a quenelle of each mousse onto each plate. Pour a little of the mango sauce between each quenelle of mousse. Top with the lighter raspberry sauce and then the darker raspberry sauce. Garnish with a fresh raspberry and three mint leaves.

MANGO AND GRAPE MOUSSE
Mousse des mangues et raisins

This is a simple recipe but very effective because of the unusual combination of fruits. The mango must be very ripe for the fullest flavor.

SERVES 4

1	large, ripe mango, about 1¼ pounds, peeled and diced
¾ pound	black grapes, washed, halved, and seeded
⅔ cup	low-fat natural yogurt (see page 31)
¾ cup	quark (see page 30)
2 tablespoons	superfine sugar
1 ounce	slivered almonds, toasted

○ Reserve some mango and a few grapes for the decoration.

○ Add the remainder to a mixture of the yogurt, quark, and sugar. Mix in well.

○ Chill for about 2 hours.

○ Stir in the almonds, then spoon into four individual glasses. Decorate with the reserved fruit and serve immediately.

DATE AND APPLE MOUSSE
Mousse de dattes et pommes fruits

Toast the pine nuts on a baking sheet in the oven to bring out their nutty taste. This is a very simple but effective recipe.

SERVES 4

1½ pounds	cooking apples, peeled, cored, and sliced
1½ tablespoons	lemon juice
3 to 5 tablespoons	honey
6 ounces	fresh dates
1 tablespoon	pine nuts, toasted
4	mint sprigs to decorate

○ Place the apple slices in a pan with the lemon juice and 2 tablespoons water. Cover and cook over very gentle heat for 10 to 15 minutes until soft, stirring occasionally.

○ Strain the apples to make a smooth purée, then stir in the honey to taste.

○ Peel and pit the dates. Cut into thin strips. Stir into the apple purée.

○ Chill the purée, if desired, or serve lukewarm in glasses, sprinkled with pine nuts and decorated with mint sprigs.

SUMMER FRUITS
WITH VANILLA SAUCE
Délice des fruits d'été

This recipe can be made with any fruit—red or black cherries, strawberries, loganberries, blueberries—and instead of the vanilla sauce, you could serve quark. It looks pretty served in goblets.

SERVES 10

1 pint	raspberries
1 pint	blackberries
½ pint	gooseberries
½ pint	red currants
½ pint	yellow currants
½ cup	sugar
6 tablespoons	cornstarch

Red berry juice:

1 pint	raspberries
1 pint	red currants
2½ cups	water

Vanilla sauce:

2	egg yolks
4 teaspoons	sugar
1⅛ cups	skim milk
1	vanilla bean, split

○ Wash the berries only if necessary. Rinse in a strainer a few at a time, allow to drain, and dry with kitchen towels.

○ Remove the stems from the berries.

○ To make the red berry juice, bring the raspberries, currants, and water to the boil, then simmer over gentle heat for 5 minutes. Push the berries through a strainer.

○ Boil the red berry juice and the ½ cup sugar until the sugar has dissolved.

○ Mix the cornstarch with 2 tablespoons water and mix into the berry juice, stirring constantly.

○ Add the prepared berries and allow to simmer for 5 minutes on the lowest heat. Cool a little.

○ Put the fruit into a glass bowl and sprinkle the surface with a little extra sugar (to prevent a skin forming). Allow to cool and place in the refrigerator.

○ To make the vanilla sauce, beat together the egg yolks and sugar until creamy. Heat the milk and vanilla bean in a pan, scrape the seeds out into the milk, and pour the milk into the egg yolks, beating all the time.

○ Pour the egg mixture back into the pan and, stirring all the time, heat until just below the boiling point. Allow the sauce to cool, then remove the vanilla bean.

○ Serve spooned onto individual plates, with a spoonful of the vanilla sauce on top.

TERRINE OF ORANGES
WITH RASPBERRY SAUCE
Pavé d'oranges à la sauce framboise

To turn the terrine out of its dish once set, dip the base of the dish
carefully into hot water, then place a plate over the top and invert.
You could use orange juice in this recipe instead of apple juice for a
more concentrated orange flavor.

SERVES 15

18	medium oranges
5⅓ tablespoons	gelatin
2½ cups	clear apple juice
1	bunch of fresh mint leaves
8 teaspoons	grenadine syrup
½ cup	water
15	tiny mint sprigs for garnish
	Fresh raspberries for garnish

Raspberry sauce:

1 quart	raspberries
4 tablespoons	confectioner's sugar
1 tablespoon	lemon juice

○ Pare the zest from three washed oranges and cut into thin julienne strips. Reserve. Squeeze the juice from these oranges.

○ Cut away the remaining peel and white pith from all the remaining oranges and carefully remove the orange segments. Remove seeds. Reserve the juice from the segmenting, add it to the other juices, and strain it through a fine strainer.

○ Dissolve the gelatin in a little warm apple juice, then add to the remaining apple juice.

○ Add ½ cup of the strained orange juice to the apple juice.

○ Chill a 1½-quart china or glass terrine dish and spoon about ¼ inch of juice into it. Chill until set, then overlap some mint leaves to cover the jelled mixture entirely.

○ Place the terrine in a large bowl of ice. Spoon a little jelled apple juice over each side in turn and press mint leaves onto each side. Chill until firm between each application.

○ Arrange half the orange segments on top of the mint leaves and spoon half the remaining juice over. Chill until set.

○ Arrange the remaining half of the orange segments on top and spoon the remaining juice over. Chill until set.

○ Place the orange zest julienne in a saucepan with the grenadine syrup and water and simmer gently until almost all the liquid has evaporated and the orange strips have turned pink. Let cool. Add a little extra water if they become too syrupy.

○ To make the sauce, purée the fresh raspberries, then strain through a sieve. Stir in the sugar and lemon juice.

○ To serve, carefully turn the terrine out of the dish, and very carefully slice. Spoon a little of the raspberry sauce onto each plate and center a slice of the terrine on top. Decorate with orange julienne, a sprig of mint, and a raspberry.

TIMBALE OF CHERRIES
WITH ORANGE SAUCE
Timbale de cerises à la sauce d'orange

SERVES 4

5 ounces	black cherries, pitted
2 tablespoons	superfine sugar
⅝ cup	low-fat natural yogurt (see page 31)
½ ounce	gelatin
⅞ cup	quark (see page 30)
8	fresh cherries, for decoration

Orange sauce:

⅔ cup	fresh orange juice
2 tablespoons	superfine sugar
	Zest of 1 orange, cut in thin julienne strips

○ Purée the cherries with the sugar in a food processor or blender.

○ Stir in the yogurt until well mixed.

○ Soften the gelatin in 2 tablespoons water, heat gently until dissolved, and stir into the cherry mixture.

○ Whisk in the quark, then pour into four individual molds and chill until set.

○ To make the sauce, place the orange juice, sugar, and orange julienne in a saucepan. Heat gently until the sugar dissolves, then simmer until reduced to about ½ cup. Cool.

○ Unmold the cherry timbales onto individual plates, spoon a little sauce around each one, and decorate with fresh cherries.

SUMMER PUDDING LYN HALL

This dish is named for the many-talented principal of La Petite Cuisine School of Cooking. She helped with the photographs for this book, and in many other ways, and I am extremely grateful for her friendship and advice.

Summer Pudding can also be prepared in individual molds—see the photograph facing page 226. If desired, sprinkle the edge of the plate with confectioner's sugar, which is a simple and exciting way of enhancing the presentation. If the fruit is at its best in flavor there is no need for added sugar in this simple and good recipe.

SERVES 4

8	thin, large slices of whole wheat bread, crusts removed, and cut into rectangles
¼ ounce	gelatin
½ cup	water
	Juice of ½ lemon
1¼ cups	ripe strawberries
1¼ cups	ripe raspberries
1¼ cups	ripe blackberries
½ cup	quark, mixed with sufficient skim milk to give a thick pouring consistency (see page 30)

Raspberry sauce:

2½ cups	raspberries
4 tablespoons	confectioner's sugar
	Juice of 1 small lemon

Decoration:

4	pairs of cherries on the stem
4	raspberries
16	blueberries
4	sprigs of mint
1 tablespoon	confectioner's sugar

○ Line a 4-cup mold with some of the rectangular slices of bread.

○ Dissolve the gelatin in the water over gentle heat, then stir in the lemon juice.

○ Strain and divide the gelatin liquid between three small saucepans.

○ Add the strawberries, raspberries, and blackberries separately to these three amounts of liquid and stew gently until just tender.

○ Place alternate layers of fruit and bread in the mold, finishing with a layer of bread.

○ Make a hole in the center and pour in any remaining fruit juice.

○ Cover with a saucer and weight down with something heavy. Allow to set in the refrigerator for a few hours.

○ For the sauce, press the raspberries through a sieve and mix with the remaining ingredients.

○ Unmold the pudding onto a serving plate and carefully pour the raspberry sauce over the top of the pudding to cover it completely.

○ Decorate with fruit and sprinkle with confectioner's sugar.

○ Fill a small parchment piping bag with the mixed quark and milk and snip off the end.

○ Pipe a circle of sauce around the outside edge, then draw a skewer through the sauce to give a decorative finish.

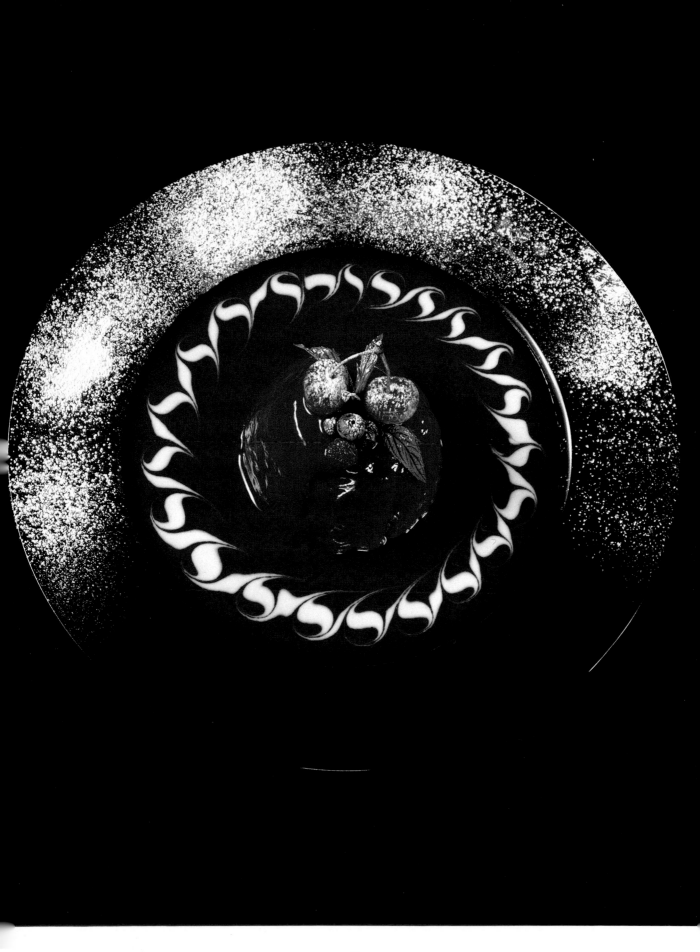

SMALL FRUIT BASKETS WITH RASPBERRY AND PEACH SAUCES

Tuiles aux amandes aux fruits de la saison

The fruits for these baskets can be varied according to season and, as they are uncooked, they retain the maximum amount of vitamin C.
You could fill the baskets with exotic fruits instead of the above summer fruits: use about 4½ cups sliced papaya, pineapple, kiwi fruit, mango, and lychees. Serve the raspberry sauce with some low-fat natural yogurt instead of the peach sauce.

SERVES 4

¾ cup	confectioner's sugar, sifted
¾ cup	all-purpose flour
3	large egg whites
	A pinch of salt
	Finely grated zest of 1½ oranges
1 ounce	slivered almonds
2½ pints	(4½ to 5 cups) mixed berries, ripe and at their best (such as raspberries, blackberries, blueberries, strawberries, red or white currants, wild strawberries, loganberries, or gooseberries)
1 tablespoon	confectioner's sugar for garnish

Raspberry sauce:

Generous ½ pint	raspberries
1 tablespoon	confectioner's sugar
	Juice of ½ lemon

Peach sauce:

½ pound	very ripe peaches, halved, pitted, and chopped
1	vanilla bean, split
3 tablespoons	water
	Juice of ½ lemon
⅝ cup	low-fat natural yogurt (see page 31)

○ Mix together the sugar, flour, egg whites, and salt to make a thick batter. Strain the mixture if necessary.

○ Add the orange zest and almonds and allow the mixture to rest for 2 hours.

○ With your fingers, spread the mixture into four 7-inch circles on nonstick baking sheets. Do not aim for perfect circles; I much prefer a ragged, wild look (see color plate, page 228).

○ Bake in a preheated oven at 350° F for about 8 minutes until golden.

○ Remove from the baking sheets immediately and place each circle on top of an inverted cup or small bowl so that it droops into a rough basket shape. Leave until cold and firm. Place in an airtight tin.

○ For the raspberry sauce, purée and strain the raspberries, then add the sugar and lemon juice. Bring to the boil, and let cool.

○ For the peach sauce, cook the peaches with the vanilla bean, water, and lemon juice for about 5 to 7 minutes until soft. Add the natural yogurt and mix well. Purée and strain. Let cool.

○ Sprinkle the confectioner's sugar over the baskets and arrange the mixed fruits in the baskets.

○ Cover individual plates with peach sauce first, then add the basket with the fruits. Garnish with the raspberry sauce to your own design.

SNOW EGGS
IN VANILLA SAUCE CHRISTIANE
Oeufs à la neige Christiane

This recipe is dedicated to Christiane Schröder, who helped with many of the dessert recipes. Her immense talent brought to life many of my ideas.

SERVES 4

3	egg whites
1 tablespoon	superfine sugar
	Dash of lemon juice
2 tablespoons	warm toasted slivered almonds, to garnish

Vanilla sauce:

1⅓ cups	skim milk
1	vanilla bean
3	egg yolks
2 tablespoons	sugar
⅝ cup	low-fat natural yogurt (see page 31)

Caramel:

4 tablespoons	superfine sugar
2 tablespoons	water

○ To make the snow eggs, whisk the egg whites until stiff. Continue whisking, adding a little sugar at a time. Whisk in the lemon juice and continue whisking until stiff.

○ Heat the milk in a large shallow pan with the vanilla bean. Spoon or pipe twelve snow eggs into the milk. Simmer very gently for about 4 minutes. Drain carefully into a clean dish towel.

○ Whisk the egg yolks and sugar together. Pour the hot milk over.

○ Place the egg mixture in a double boiler or bowl over a pan of simmering water and cook until the mixture thickens sufficiently to coat the back of a wooden spoon. Cool slightly.

○ Stir in the yogurt. Strain and keep warm.

○ For the caramel, dissolve the sugar in the water over gentle heat. Boil to a golden caramel, then drizzle decoratively onto a nonstick baking sheet to make twelve caramel garnishes.

○ To serve, pour the vanilla sauce into four individual soup plates. Arrange three snow eggs in each plate. Top with caramel and sprinkle with warm toasted almonds (see photograph oppposite). Serve immediately.

CARROT AND HONEY CAKE
Pain de carottes et miel

This cake, rich in vitamin A, can be served at teatime as well as for dessert.

SERVES 4

2	eggs, separated
3½ tablespoons	clear honey
	Grated zest and juice of ½ large *or* 1 small lemon
¼ pound	(2 medium) carrots, peeled and finely grated
4 ounces	hazelnuts, very coarsely ground
	A generous pinch of ground cinnamon
	A pinch of ground cloves
1 ounce	whole wheat grains, finely milled into flour (see discussion on page 243)

○ Whisk together the egg yolks, honey, lemon zest, and juice until frothy.

○ Stir in the carrots, hazelnuts, spices, and flour.

○ Whisk the egg whites until stiff, then fold into the carrot mixture.

○ Transfer to an ovenproof dish and bake in the oven at 350° F for 20 to 25 minutes until risen and golden and firm to the touch.

WALNUT CHEESECAKE

This is the Cuisine Naturelle version of cheesecake, baked without the conventional cookie-crumb-and-butter base.

SERVES 10

3 cups	yogurt curd cheese (see page 32)
½ cup	light brown sugar
3	eggs, beaten
4 ounces	shelled walnuts, chopped
2 tablespoons	all-purpose flour
10	walnut halves, for garnish

○ Beat together the yogurt curd cheese, sugar, eggs, walnuts, and flour until evenly mixed. Pour into a 9-inch springform pan lined with parchment or wax paper.

○ Bake in the oven at 350° F for about 40 minutes until set. Allow to cool, then remove from the pan.

○ Garnish with the walnuts.

RASPBERRY STRUDEL
Strudel de framboises

SERVES 8

8 ounces	filo dough (see page 34)
¼ cup	water
1 tablespoon	confectioner's sugar

Filling:

2½ pints	fresh raspberries (or blackberries)
4 tablespoons	superfine sugar
4 ounces	toasted hazelnuts, ground

○ Be sure that the pastry is very thin, and cut it into rectangular sheets of about 12 × 24 inches.

○ Warm the water and confectioner's sugar together.

○ Layer the filo rectangles, brushing each sheet with the sweetened water.

○ Sprinkle the raspberries with the sugar.

○ Sprinkle the pastry with the ground hazelnuts and top with the raspberries.

○ Fold in the two long edges of the pastry, then, with the help of a cloth, roll up the strudel from a short edge.

○ Place seam side down on a nonstick baking sheet. Bake in the oven at 400° F for about 25 minutes until golden.

○ Dust with a little extra confectioner's sugar before serving, sliced on the diagonal.

ALMOND COOKIES
Biscuits d'amandes

MAKES 40 COOKIES

4	egg whites
½ cup	superfine sugar
5 ounces	ground almonds
40	blanched almond halves

○ Whisk the egg whites until stiff.

○ Whisk the sugar into the egg whites, a little at a time.

○ Fold in the ground almonds.

○ Place the mixture in a pastry bag and pipe little whirls onto nonstick baking sheets. Top each one with an almond half.

○ Bake in the oven at 350° F for about 20 to 25 minutes until golden. Cool on a wire rack.

DATE PETITS FOURS
Petits fours aux dattes

Dates contain fiber and some calcium, iron, and niacin (one of the B vitamins).

MAKES 24

11 ounces	fresh dates, pitted
4 ounces	toasted hazelnuts, skinned
2 tablespoons	thick pear juice or apple cider

○ Finely chop the dates and hazelnuts.

○ Mix together with sufficient juice to bind them.

○ Shape into twenty-four small ovals and place in petits fours cups.

SESAME PETITS FOURS

Petits fours au sésame

MAKES 24 PIECES

1	egg
3 tablespoons	superfine sugar
½ cup	whole wheat flour
⅓ cup	sesame seeds
	Grated rind of ½ lemon
	A little milk (if necessary)

○ Whisk together the egg and sugar until frothy.

○ Add the remaining ingredients and knead to a firm dough, adding a little milk if necessary.

○ Roll out the dough as thinly as possible on a lightly floured board and cut out 2½-inch rounds.

○ Transfer to a nonstick baking tray and bake in the oven at 350° F for about 15 minutes until golden.

○ Allow to cool for a few moments before transferring to a cooling rack. Let cool completely.

OAT COCKTAIL WITH FRESH FRUITS
Cocktail vital

This can be served as an hors d'oeuvre, but here it makes a healthful dessert. Any kind or mixture of fruit can be used.

SERVES 4

4 tablespoons	rolled oats
½ cup	warmed skim milk
⅝ cup	low-fat natural yogurt (see page 31)
4 tablespoons	honey
2 tablespoons	lemon juice
2	apples, 1 red and 1 green, washed and cored
4½ to 5 cups	berries (strawberries, raspberries, red currants, blackberries, blueberries, depending on the season)
4 tablespoons	hazelnuts, toasted, skinned, and chopped
4	sprigs of fresh mint
4	raspberries for garnish

○ Soak the rolled oats for 15 minutes in the warm milk, then mix with the yogurt, honey, and lemon juice.

○ Grate the apples and add to the mixture.

○ Cut up the berries (if necessary) and add to the mixture.

○ Mix in the chopped nuts and serve garnished with the mint and raspberries.

POACHED FIGS WITH MINT SABAYON

Figues pochées au sabayon de menthe

SERVES 4

4 tablespoons	superfine sugar
1⅛ cups	water
4	sprigs of mint, well washed
16	small fresh figs, carefully peeled
2	egg yolks
1 teaspoon	freshly chopped mint
	Mint sprigs to garnish

○ Heat the sugar in a pan with a little extra water and boil steadily until caramelized. Remove from the heat and very carefully add the measured water.

○ Add the four washed sprigs of mint and simmer gently, stirring occasionally, until the caramel dissolves.

○ Add the peeled figs to the pan and cook for 1 to 2 minutes until just soft. Remove from the heat.

○ Remove the figs from the pan and allow to cool.

○ Strain the caramel syrup into a clean pan and boil to reduce to ⅔ cup. Cool.

○ Beat together the egg yolks, whisk in the caramel syrup, then continue to whisk in a bowl over a pan of simmering water until thick and frothy. Stir in the chopped mint.

○ Spoon the warm sabayon sauce onto four plates, arrange the figs on top, and garnish with mint leaves.

SEASONAL FRUIT TERRINE, JANET

Poésie de fruits en terrine, Janet

I could not have evolved the ideas of Cuisine Naturelle without the enthusiastic and generous help of Dr. Janet Gale, to whom this recipe is dedicated. I cannot thank her enough.

SERVES 15

5⅓ tablespoons	gelatin
2½ cups	clear white grape juice
1	bunch of fresh peppermint
About ⅔ cup	sliced mango
Generous ½ pint	raspberries or strawberries, sliced
About 1⅓ cups	sliced papaya
½ pint	blueberries
¼ pound	black or green grapes, halved and seeded
	Slices of extra fruit and mint sprigs to decorate

Raspberry sauce:

Scant 1½ pints	raspberries, puréed and strained
2 tablespoons	confectioner's sugar
	Juice of 1 small lemon

○ Dissolve the gelatin in a little of the warmed grape juice. Add the remaining grape juice and let cool.

○ Surround a 1½-quart china or glass terrine dish with ice. Pour a little of the grape juice into it. Allow to set, then arrange peppermint leaves over the jelled mixture.

○ Turn the terrine onto its side and coat that side with a little of the grape juice. Allow to set and arrange mint leaves over. Repeat on the other sides.

○ Place the fruit in layers in the terrine, pouring a little of the juice over each layer and allowing it to set before continuing with the next layer.

○ Chill the terrine for 2 to 3 hours until set.

○ To make the raspberry sauce, mix the puréed raspberries with the sugar and lemon juice. Chill.

○ To serve, turn the terrine out carefully onto a dish (dip the terrine briefly into hot water to loosen) and slice. Serve decorated with fresh fruit, raspberry sauce, and mint sprigs.

BREADS

Homemade bread has very special memories for me. I was brought up, literally, in a restaurant kitchen, and the most potent fragrance of my childhood was that of bread baking in the wood-fired ovens. Even today, the unmistakable smell of baking bread evokes clear and powerful images, and the wonderful taste it had is still in my mind. Not surprisingly, I have a very special love for good, freshly made, tasty bread.

Bread is one of the world's oldest foods, as well as one of the healthiest. White bread—now somewhat less popular than it used to be—nevertheless provides some protein and B vitamins as well as minerals (particularly calcium) and trace elements. Whole wheat bread contains all these (except calcium) and a slightly higher proportion of vitamins and iron, as well as fiber from the bran content of the whole wheat flour.

Whole wheat—literally the whole grain, outer layer and kernel—is undoubtedly better for health and can be eaten as cereal in granola and as flour in bread, rolls, and cakes. Whole wheat, in whatever form, is digested slowly, and as a result, one's appetite is satisfied promptly, and this feeling lasts for a long period of time. Whole wheat grains, known as wheat berries, are becoming more widely available and, for the greatest benefit, should be milled just before use (light and air, as with vegetables, affect the nutrients in the grains). Hand and electric mills are available for use in the home (or a good strong coffee grinder), but failing this, buy the best whole wheat flour in small amounts and often to ensure quality and freshness. And always, after sifting, use the bran left in the sifter.

Other grains and cereals are valuable nutritionally, and rye, millet, barley, and corn can all be used in bread making. The corn breads in this chapter are light and tasty.

MINT AND POPPY SEED BREAD

This bread can be served with salads or main courses.

MAKES 1 SMALL ROUND LOAF, TO SERVE 10

11 ounces	whole wheat grains, finely milled into flour
2	pinches of salt
1 tablespoon	celery seeds
1 tablespoon	poppy seeds
1 tablespoon	freshly cut fresh mint
½ ounce	fresh yeast
1 cup	tepid water
1	egg, beaten, to glaze

○ Mix together the flour, salt, celery and poppy seeds, and mint in a bowl.

○ Mix the yeast with ¼ cup of the water and leave for 10 minutes or so until frothy.

○ Mix the yeast into the flour with the remaining water to make a soft dough.

○ Knead on a lightly floured surface for 10 minutes, then shape into a round.

○ Place on a nonstick baking sheet, cover with a damp cloth, and leave in a warm place until doubled in size—about 25 to 30 minutes.

○ Lightly brush with beaten egg and bake in the oven at 400° F for about 30 minutes. To test if the bread is baked, tap the base. It will sound hollow when done.

SAVORY SESAME BISCUITS
Biscuits à sésame

These savory biscuits can be served instead of bread with salads and cheese.

MAKES 24 PIECES

1 pound	whole wheat grains, finely milled into flour
⅓ cup	rye flakes
2	pinches of salt
½ teaspoon	ground coriander
½ ounce	fresh yeast
1⅓ cups	lukewarm water
⅓ cup	sesame seeds
1	egg, beaten

○ Mix together the flour, rye flakes, salt, and ground coriander.

○ Mix yeast and water. Gradually work into the flour mixture to make a firm dough.

○ Sprinkle the work surface with half the sesame seeds and knead the dough on it until all the seeds are incorporated and the dough is firm and workable. Cover with a damp dish towel and let rise for 30 minutes.

○ Roll the dough out on a lightly floured surface to a rectangle 12 x 16 inches. Lay on a nonstick baking sheet.

○ With a sharp, wet knife, mark the dough into twenty-four rectangles, 2 x 4 inches. Prick the dough with a fork, brush with the beaten egg, and sprinkle with the remaining sesame seeds.

○ Bake in the oven at 400° F for 15 to 20 minutes until crisp and golden. Break apart and serve warm.

CARROT AND ZUCCHINI MUFFINS

Serve warm for a savory and healthy breakfast.

MAKES 24 MUFFINS

½ pound	whole wheat grains, finely milled into flour
½ cup	all-purpose flour
1 teaspoon	baking powder
1 teaspoon	ground cinnamon
½ teaspoon	ground allspice
½ teaspoon	ground nutmeg
½ teaspoon	salt
3	eggs
6 to 7 tablespoons	clear honey
½ cup	skim milk
1	small orange, all peel and pith removed, segmented and chopped
¼	vanilla bean, split and center scraped out
1½ cups	grated carrots
1½ cups	grated zucchini
2 ounces	shelled walnuts, coarsely chopped

○ Sift the dry ingredients into a bowl. Add the bran from the sifter.

○ Whisk together the eggs, honey, and milk.

○ Combine all the ingredients, including the black vanilla seeds. Beat well until evenly mixed, then divide between twenty-four nonstick muffin cups.

○ Bake at 400° F for about 15 minutes until risen and golden.

FLOWERPOT BREAD WITH ONIONS
Pain en pot à fleurs aux oignons

Flowerpots make good baking molds. Wash new clay flowerpots and allow to dry well. Heat the pots on a baking sheet for 30 minutes at 425° F. They will give off a lot of smoke! Allow to cool.

MAKES 2 LOAVES, ENOUGH FOR 12 TO 16 PEOPLE

1 pound	all-purpose flour, plus flour for sprinkling and kneading
2	pinches of sugar
2	pinches of salt
½ ounce	fresh yeast
¾ cup	lukewarm skim milk
9 tablespoons	lukewarm water
1	medium onion, grated

○ Sift 1 pound of the flour, the sugar, and the salt into a bowl.

○ Mix the fresh yeast with a little lukewarm milk, then add the remaining liquids.

○ Work in half the measured flour, sprinkle with a little of the extra flour, then cover the bowl with a damp dish towel and leave in a warm place for 15 minutes to rise.

○ Work the remaining half of the flour into the risen dough until it comes away from the sides of the bowl.

○ On a lightly floured board knead the dough for 10 to 15 minutes until smooth and shiny.

○ Sprinkle a bowl with flour and place the dough in it. Cover with a damp cloth and leave to rise in a warm place for 1 to 1½ hours.

○ Meanwhile, sauté the onion lightly in a nonstick pan. Add the onion to the risen dough and knead well.

○ Divide the dough into two even pieces. Knead each piece into a ball and place in a foil-lined clay flowerpot about 5 to 6 inches in diameter.

○ Cover the flowerpots and leave to rise again for 30 minutes.

○ Bake in a preheated oven at 375° F for about 40 minutes until well browned.

○ To test if the bread is baked, remove from the pot and tap the base. It will sound hollow when done.

CORN BREAD
Pain de maïs

Because cornmeal is a soft flour, it is usually mixed with another flour
to give the best results.

SERVES 10

1 cup plus 2 tablespoons	cornmeal
¾ cup	whole wheat flour
2 teaspoons	baking powder
	A pinch of salt
⅓ cup	cottage cheese
1 cup	skim milk
1	egg

○ Sift the cornmeal, flour, baking powder, and salt into a mixing bowl.

○ Beat the cottage cheese, milk, and egg together and stir into the flour mixture.

○ Turn the mixture into an 8-inch square cake pan, lined with parchment or wax paper, and bake in the oven at 400° F for 20 to 25 minutes until risen and firm to the touch.

○ Cool slightly, then cut into sixteen squares. Serve warm with honey.

PICNIC FRUIT BREAD
Pain pique-nique

This fruit loaf is delicious for breakfast or merely as a snack.

MAKES 1 LOAF, TO SERVE 10

¾ pound	whole wheat grains, finely milled into flour
	A pinch of salt
½ ounce	fresh yeast
1 tablespoon	fromage blanc (see page 29)
1 cup	tepid water
1	egg, beaten, to glaze

Filling

¼ cup	dried pears or apricots
3 ounces	hazelnuts, toasted, skinned, and coarsely chopped
4 tablespoons	candied citrus
5 tablespoons	sultanas or raisins
	Grated zest of ½ lemon

○ Place the flour and salt in a bowl.

○ Mix the yeast, fromage blanc, and about ¼ cup of the water. Leave for 5 to 10 minutes until frothy.

○ Add the yeast mixture and remaining water to the flour. Mix well to a smooth dough, then knead on a lightly floured surface for about 10 minutes.

○ Place in a bowl, cover with a damp cloth or plastic wrap, and leave in a warm place until doubled in size, about 40 minutes.

○ Meanwhile, prepare the filling. Soak the dried pears or apricots in hot water for 15 minutes. Drain and dry and cut into small pieces. Combine with the remaining filling ingredients.

○ Remove the dough from the bowl and knead well. Divide into one-third and two-thirds.

○ Knead all the filling ingredients into the two-thirds of dough and shape into a roll about 9 inches long.

○ On a lightly floured surface roll out the remaining dough to a rectangle large enough to encase the fruit roll.

○ Place the fruit roll in the center of the dough and wrap the dough around to enclose it completely.

- Place seam side down in a 2-pound nonstick or foil-lined loaf pan.

- Cover with a damp cloth and leave in a warm place to rise until the dough completely fills the pan.

- Brush very carefully with beaten egg, then bake in the oven at 375° F for 35 to 40 minutes until golden brown. To test if completely baked, remove bread from pan and tap the base. It will sound hollow when done.

WHOLE WHEAT MUFFINS

Serve warm at breakfast or teatime.

MAKES 16 MUFFINS

11 ounces	whole wheat grains, finely milled into flour
2 teaspoons	baking powder
	A pinch of salt
2	eggs
1 cup	skim milk
2 tablespoons	honey

- Sift flour, baking powder, and salt into a bowl. Add bran from sifter.

- Whisk together eggs, milk, and warmed honey.

- Combine all the ingredients and beat well until evenly mixed.

- Divide mixture among 16 nonstick muffin cups and bake for about 15 minutes in a preheated oven at 400° F until risen and golden.

CORN CAKE WITH PLUMS
Gâteau de maïs aux pruneaux

These plum squares are delicious for breakfast or to accompany morning coffee or afternoon tea. You could use apricots instead of the plums.

SERVES 10

1 cup	cornmeal
¾ cup	whole wheat flour
1½ teaspoons	baking powder
4 ounces	clear honey
1	egg, beaten
	Finely grated zest of 1 small lemon
4 to 5 tablespoons	skim milk, to mix
About 1 pound	plums, washed
	Confectioner's sugar to garnish

○ Stir together the cornmeal, flour, and baking powder in a bowl.

○ Add the honey, egg, and lemon rind, then stir in sufficient milk to mix to a soft dough.

○ Press the dough gently into a 7-by-11-inch cake pan, lined with wax or parchment paper.

○ Halve and pit the plums and place, cut side down, on the dough.

○ Bake in the oven at 375° F for 20 to 25 minutes.

○ Sprinkle with confectioner's sugar, then serve warm, cut in squares.

GLOSSARY

Al dente Usually applied to vegetables and pasta that are slightly undercooked so that they are crunchy or have some resilience to the bite.

Bain-marie A roasting or baking pan half-filled with hot water in which terrines, custards, and the like stand. The food is protected from fierce direct heat and poaches in a gentle, steamy atmosphere. It is also used for keeping foods warm without the contents being spoiled by overheating or dryness. A double boiler on top of the stove serves a similar purpose.

Bouquet garni Can be changed according to needs of recipe, but usually a mixture of parsley stems, bay leaf, peppercorns, and thyme wrapped with celeriac and carrots and tied together.

A white bouquet garni consists only of onion, white of leek, and celeriac plus herbs. It is used for white stocks.

Concasser To chop finely or pound in a mortar. With tomatoes, peel, seed, and dice finely.

Coulis A liquid purée of fruit or vegetables, usually tomatoes, made without flour.

Court bouillon A seasoned liquid or stock in which to poach fish or shellfish.

Dress To pluck, draw (gut), and truss poultry and game.

Emincer To cut into small slices.

Escalope A thin slice of meat, usually veal, sometimes beaten out flat to make thinner and larger. This technique may be applied to poultry and some fish.

Fillet A prime cut of meat, fish, or poultry, with all bones removed.

Fromage blanc *Fromage frais* ("fresh cheese") in France, for which there is no direct American equivalent, unless homemade (see page 29). Cottage cheese is too granular, and cream cheese has a more cloying texture. Fromage blanc has a light consistency, like thick drained yogurt (from which a curd cheese can be made as well, see page 32).

Garnish An edible decoration added to savory and sweet dishes to improve appearance, to awaken tastes, and to add variety or color.

Glace de viande A good stock reduced to a glaze, for adding body and color to sauces, prepared by reducing a basic beef, veal, or lamb stock (see page 25). Poultry, game, and fish stocks can be reduced to a glaze as well.

Glaze To cover—to improve appearance, by adding a gloss—with a thin layer of reduced meat, poultry, or fish stock (for savory dishes), milk or beaten egg (for pastries or bread), a reduction of stock or juices (for vegetables).

Julienne Meats, vegetables, or citrus peel cut into long, thin strands like matchsticks, not longer than the width of a soup spoon.

Mandoline A metal or wood frame with adjustable blades set in it for slicing vegetables finely, such as potatoes, cucumbers, and the like.

Marinade A seasoned liquid in which to soak fish, meat, or vegetables before further preparation to give flavor and tenderize.

Medallions Small rounds of meat, game, fish, or shellfish, evenly cut. A *mignon* is similar.

Mirepoix The vegetable equivalent of a bouquet garni, often used as an aromatic bed for stews. It consists of roughly chopped vegetables (size according to need and whether mirepoix is to be discarded or used as a garnish), usually carrots, onions, and celery, but turnips or other vegetables, plus herbs, can be added as well.

A white mirepoix, for a white stock or sauce, consists of onions, white of leek, celeriac, and added herbs.

Nutrients They are proteins, fats, carbohydrates, minerals, and vitamins. These, even including a proportion of fat, are vital for good health. Fiber, although not strictly speaking a nutrient, is also necessary. All are available for the use of the body from fresh, well-prepared food.

Oven temperatures The following are roughly equivalent oven dial markings, not exact conversions.

Description	Degrees Celsius	Degrees Fahrenheit
Very cool	110	225
	120	250
Cool	140	275
	150	300
Moderate	160	325
	180	350
Moderately hot	190	375
	200	400
Hot	220	425
	230	450
Very hot	240	475

en Papillote Literally "in envelope." A wrapping of paper or foil in which fish or meat is baked so as to contain aroma and flavor.

Petits fours Very small fancy cakes or biscuits served after a meal, usually with coffee.

Quenelles Most commonly, a light dumpling mixture of finely minced meat, fish, poultry, or game—and egg whites—to be poached. A quenelle should be shaped like an egg between two warm tablespoons.

Suprême Choice pieces of poultry or game birds, usually the breast, and fish.

Terrine A china, earthenware, glass, metal, or foil dish used for pâtés and some desserts. The word also applies to the foods baked or molded in the terrine.

Timbale A thimble-shaped (but not -sized) mold for the preparation of savory or sweet mixtures.

Tofu A "curd cheese" made from soybean milk, known as *tofu* in Japan, but of Chinese origin. It has almost no taste of its own but is rich in nutrients—the soybean is the richest natural vegetable food known to man.

Yogurt Yogurt is formed from cow's, sheep's, or goat's milk by the addition and action of benevolent bacilli. It is digested more rapidly and easily than milk, and its mild acidity is good for the stomach. It is a satisfying food and is low in calories, especially when made with skim milk (see page 31).

INDEX

Anton Mosimann, a fourth-generation chef, was born in Solothurn, Switzerland, in 1947. He has trained and worked in Italy, Canada, and Japan, as well as his native Switzerland, and in 1976, when he was still only twenty-nine, he was appointed Maître-Chef des Cuisines at London's Dorchester Hotel. He is considered to be one of the finest chefs working anywhere in the world today; his skill, innovation, and energy have brought accolades to the Dorchester's two restaurants, The Terrace and The Dorchester Grill Room, both of which feature Cuisine Naturelle dishes on their menus.